English coursework
Modern Drama

Margaret K. Gray has an hono... University and a Ph.D. from G... had wide teaching experience in secondary schools, further education college, and university. She has been an examiner for the Scottish Certificate of Education Board at O grade, and tutored extensively at CSE and A level. She is the editor of *Selected Short Stories of the Supernatural* by Margaret Oliphant (Scottish Academic Press) and is a regular contributor to many journals.

Also available:

English coursework: Prose
English coursework: Drama and Poetry
English coursework: Conflict
English coursework: Women and Society
English coursework: Childhood and Adolescence
English coursework: Science Fiction
English coursework: Modern Poetry

Brodie's Notes on

English coursework

Modern Drama

M. K. Gray BA Ph.D

Pan Books London, Sydney and Auckland

First published 1991 by
Pan Books Ltd, Cavaye Place, London SW10 9PG

9 8 7 6 5 4 3 2 1

© Pan Books Ltd 1991

ISBN 0 330 50330 8

Photoset by Parker Typesetting Service, Leicester

Printed in England by Clays Ltd, St Ives plc

Modern Drama

Dramatists and plays referred to in this book

See p.108 for a list of individual Brodie's Notes on some of the above texts. These will help you with details on your coursework *and* increase your knowledge of the play concerned.

Contents

Preface by the general editor

The thematic approach to the study of literature has long been practised by teachers, and this new series of Brodie's Notes focuses on areas of investigation which will help teachers and students at GCSE and A-level alike.

The Notes will stimulate disciplined and imaginative involvement with your chosen books by widening your horizons to the possibility of studying works which are comparable in theme (say, Conflict) or genre (say, the Short Story).

Do not get so absorbed that you see *only* the theme under discussion and nothing else: the theme of any book – whether the presentation of marriage, or of love, or of conflict – is only a part of the whole. Read primarily to enjoy and discover, and try to work out how important the theme you are examining is to the whole: it may reside in character or situation or social conditions or any number of areas. One thing is sure: by recognizing and appreciating the theme or themes you will have learned more about the work you are studying. As a result you will be able to write about it more fully, and place it in a broader literary context.

The editor of each Theme/Genre Note in this series is an experienced teacher, and his or her aim is to promote your interest in a range of ideas and books – whether prose, drama or poetry, at the same time extending your capacity for literary appreciation and your imaginative participation in what you read.

For more specific help, you can refer to Brodie's Notes on individual texts.

Graham Handley 1991

Introduction

What exactly do we mean when we speak of modern drama? We can say that we mean, at the very least, plays that have been written in recent times, but if we take that as our sole definition we are in danger of forgetting that the term 'modern' is a relative one.

For Tudor audiences Shakespeare's plays were modern, for the eighteenth century theatre-goer Sheridan's witty dramas were no less so. What we confidently label as 'modern' today are plays that will be studied and assessed by students in the twenty-first century as part of the history of the genre, plays that will undoubtedly have been superseded by *that* century's modern drama. Recentness, then, clearly cannot be taken as our only yardstick.

The Greek philosopher Aristotle, writing in the fourth century BC, stated that 'plot', 'character', a logical sequence of events, and the audience's emotional involvement were essential components of a serious play. If we look at modern drama, however, much of it apparently overturns Aristotle's premises. The plot element can be minimal or even non-existent, and apparently nonsensical incidents often replace a logical sequence of events. The barriers between tragedy and farce have been broken down. Illusion is deliberately undermined so that the audience is well aware that what it is watching is a performance. Modern drama, we might therefore say, is drama which is written in a style that is different, and original, compared to any drama that has appeared on the stage before.

The themes that modern dramatists depict also appear to be unlike any others that have been portrayed. Previously man had an unquestioning religious faith, a belief in a divinity that controlled his destiny and gave it purpose. We no longer have that certainty. Our age is an era dominated by science and by all the wonders that science has achieved, and yet science has not created paradise. We live in societies dominated by violence, isolation, uncertainty and fear. Twentieth century dramatists portray that sense of being lost, that overwhelming awareness of being purposeless and alone.

This, then, the student of drama could state, is what we mean by modern drama – the portrayal of today's world by today's dramatists, using methods never seen before, discussing themes never explored before. To assert this, however, it is necessary not only to look at examples of modern drama but also to consider some of the drama of the past.

Medieval drama and Bertolt Brecht

Medieval plays appear at first glance to contain little of interest or relevance to twentieth century drama. 'Morality plays', as they are termed, were created essentially for specific religious purposes. Some, such as *Everyman* (written probably before the end of the fifteenth century), present a grim warning to the unrepentant sinner of the dangers involved in heedlessly pursuing a self-satisfying way of life. Others, like Sir David Lindsay's *The Satire of the Three Estates* (1540), show us the court of King Humanity with its dominating vices and few virtues.

These dramas were obviously written to remind their audiences of the shortness of human life and the dangers of living a life dedicated solely to pleasure. What is also noticeable, however, is that the plays' presentations are very close to some of our own modern dramas. *Everyman* has no specific setting and reflects no particular time; the *Satire* has virtually no plot. Apart from the character of Everyman there are no 'people' in the play, only personified concepts like 'Strength', 'Beauty', 'Knowledge'. The *Satire* makes little attempt to create any illusion, as much of the story is addressed directly at the audience by the actors.

If we look at the drama of Bertolt Brecht (1898–1956) and his followers, we can see its striking relationship to these early dramatic efforts.

In what is termed *illusionistic* theatre, actors pretend to be somebody else to an audience that accepts that they *are* that someone else. In *presentational* theatre, such as the medieval moralities, the actors make no such pretence. They portray characters, personifications, ideas, to an audience, and that audience is supposed to relate what it sees to its own situation, and then alter its behaviour for the better.

Brecht called his interpretation of *presentational* theatre *alienation theatre*. Like the morality dramatists, he wished his audience to be aware that what they were watching was a play. He believed that if he could achieve this, then hopefully it would be impossible for the audience to become emotionally involved with the characters. With no emotional involvement to distract them, his audience would then be free to consider the moral and social issues he wanted them to examine. The social and moral issues were not to be presented in any black and white manner, but in such a way that audiences would be left wondering how they would have reacted if they had been in the same circumstances, what *they* would have done. Brecht and his followers are, therefore, working in the tradition of the morality plays, plays that can be seen as the forerunners of the theatre of ideas.

Chekhov, Strindberg, and the origin of modern dialogue

To present new ideas and concepts, drama required new dialogue. From the age of Shakespeare until the end of the nineteenth century, characters on stage always spoke of their hopes, dreams, and fears, much more directly and eloquently than anyone has ever done in 'real' life. No one in these plays is ever so happy or amazed or distraught that he or she is rendered inarticulate or even speechless, as is actually the case with 'ordinary' people.

It was the Swedish dramatist August Strindberg (1849–1912) who introduced realistic communication in such plays as *Miss Julie* (1888) and *The Dance of Death* (1901), having his characters talk past one another rather than at one another.

The Russian playwright Anton Chekhov (1860–1904) introduced oblique dialogue where apparently innocent words hint at hidden undercurrents of meaning. As well as introducing more realistic dialogue, Chekhov also strove for a more realistic representation on stage. In such plays as *The Seagull* (1895), *The Three Sisters* (1901), and *The Cherry Orchard* (1904) there are no superfluous characters, no stock characters, and the most commonplace incidents take on significance because they reflect the inner struggles of the central characters.

The influence of Ibsen

Drama now had a more naturalistic dialogue but it also needed a new focus, and this came from the Norwegian dramatist Heinrik Ibsen (1828–1906), who was to prove to be one of the most inspirational contributors to the modern theatre.

Ibsen set his plays in small-town society and family circles where his characters feel constricted and stifled. In his first phase in *The Pillars of the Community* (1877), *A Doll's House* (1879), *Ghosts* (1881), *The Enemy of the People* (1882), and *The Wild Duck* (1884), Ibsen exposes the effects of lies upon the individual and the individual's family, and considers the moral responsibility of the individual to the society he or she lives in.

In his second phase of *Hedda Gabler* (1908), *The Master Builder* (1892), *Little Eyolf* (1896) and *When We Dead Awaken* (1899), Ibsen turned to the effects that public life and the claims of the family had upon the inner spiritual development of the individual.

The enemies to be faced and fought in all his work are convention, hypocrisy, expedience, and past sins that influence the present. For Ibsen, the closeness and intricacy of society's structure makes it a force which threatens the fulfilment of the individual. This is not to imply that his individuals are blameless examples of idealism continually struggling against a repressive society. Ibsen's characters are flawed, intensely human. Ibsen makes no judgement on these characters or the situations they find themselves in. He simply depicts the lives of ordinary people in a small world. It was a focus that was to influence many modern dramatists. Wesker, O'Neill, Miller, Bolt and Rattigan are just a few whose work reveals that influence.

Early twentieth century dramatists

Initially the response to Ibsen's ideas in Britain was limited. George Bernard Shaw (1856–1950) was a great admirer, and attempted through such plays as *Arms and the Man* (1894) and *The Devil's Disciple* (1897) both to entertain and to depict the pressures of society. In Britain, however, he stood virtually alone.

J. M. Barrie (1860–1937) preferred to show his rather resigned view of life through the comic examination of humanity's foibles in such works as *The Admirable Crichton* (1902) and *What Every Woman Knows* (1906).

The Irish dramatist J. M. Synge (1871–1909) achieved greater realism in *The Playboy of the Western World* (1909). Certainly there are elements of farce when Christy's father is 'resurrected' and Christy becomes a kind of country Don Juan. The play, however, can also be viewed as a tragedy, thus being one of the first of this century's dramas to have not only a provincial setting but also to break down the barriers between farce and tragedy.

The influence of the First World War on drama

It was not a new British dramatist who single-handedly sharpened the focus of British drama into a consideration and examination of society, but an external, cataclysmic event.

The First World War (1914–1918) had been proclaimed as the 'war to end all wars', a chivalric confrontation between Good and Evil. The reality, however, proved to be year after year of living in rat-infested trenches, men driven half-insane by constant shelling, and butchery on an obscene scale.

No plays depicting the grim realities of the war were presented during the war years. In the men at the Front, however, the seeds of conflict were being sown, seeds of resentment and hostility towards the authorities they felt had deceived them. Authority was beginning to be questioned, and would be ultimately ferociously attacked in the drama of the nineteen fifties and sixties.

The first indication of a different perspective came from an apparently unlikely source – Harold Brighouse (1882–1958) and his provincial comedy *Hobson's Choice* (1916). Only the most acute of the audience realized that what Brighouse was portraying through comedy was the contradiction of a strong woman in a male-dominated society. Brighouse's heroine was entitled to no vote, had no rights in society, and yet possessed a far more acute business brain than any of the men in the play.

It was the Irish playwright Sean O'Casey (1880–1964) in *Juno and the Paycock* (1924) and *The Plough and the Stars* (1926) who first depicted through a blend of humour and grim tragedy the shatteringly destructive effects on ordinary people of – in this case – a civil war. The futility and horror of the First World War was only finally exposed in 1928, in *Journey's End* by R. C. Sherriff (1896–1975). What is most noticeable and most important too in *Journey's End* is not only the realistic portrayal of life in the trenches, but also the complete absence of any comforting faith. There had been no place for gentle Jesus meek and mild in the trenches, and many of the men who survived the war emerged faithless. If there was no Jesus and consequently no resurrection, however, man's purpose on earth seemed nothing more than a wretched progress towards death and oblivion.

The search for identity

Like many other people of the time, dramatists sought to find in their work a reason for man's existence. For George Bernard Shaw, whose plays — *Man and Superman* (1905), *Major Barbara* (1905), *St Joan* (1923), *The Apple Cart* (1929) — largely dominated the years from 1900 to 1930, the German philosopher Nietzsche (1844–1900) seemed to provide the answer.

Nietzsche's theory was that evolution had not ceased with the evolution of man from apeman. Eventually a new breed of supermen would evolve, men who possessed beauty and strength of form, and intelligence and nobility of mind. These men would lead the common herd unhampered by any Christian code, having created their own morality. Nietzsche was eventually to be condemned as the originator of the Nazi belief in Germanic supremacy over all other races, but initially he had many followers because he appeared to offer an alternative to Christian faith. This alternative was not rooted in God but in Man, and Shaw developed this theory into what he called the Life Force.

The dramatists J. B. Priestley, James Bridie, T. S. Eliot, Christopher Fry, and Terence Rattigan found no consolation in Nietzsche's doctrine and attempted to formulate their own theories and themes.

For J. B. Priestley (1894–1984) the interlocking chains of human responsibility were of paramount importance. What one person does or does not do affects the lives of others. Collective responsibility is the cornerstone of his work. Coupled with this message was a dramatic pre-occupation with a fourth dimension and a delving into the subconscious mind. To depict this interest, Priestley rejected the fantastic and the melodramatic in favour of ordinary, commonplace environments and people, and it is this very ordinariness that creates an eerie atmosphere in *Dangerous Corner* (1932), *Time and the Conways* (1937) and *An Inspector Calls* (1947).

For James Bridie (1888–1951) an interesting combination of

reality and intellectual debate, humour and fantasy, provides the core of his drama. There are elements of the medieval morality in such dramas as the parable *Tobias and the Angel* (1930) and the fantasy *Mr Bolfry* (1943), but Bridie's use of wit to 'sweeten the pill' of instruction occasionally blunts the impact of his message.

T. S. Eliot (1888–1965) took the medieval morality as his inspiration for the style of *Murder in the Cathedral* (1935), the historic past for its setting, added a Greek Chorus (see p. 46) as a protagonist, and created his own speech form for the play's presentation. As in the original morality plays, the theme of the ultimate human solitude at the end of life is examined. Life is shown to be essentially trivial, but for Eliot only a profound belief in God can give it any meaning. The real Hell for Eliot was to be linked to no one and nothing – a condition that would result in terrifying loneliness.

Christopher Fry (b. 1907) also set such plays as *A Phoenix Too Frequent* (1946), *Thor, With Angels* (1949), and *The Lady's Not For Burning* (1949) in the historic past but, instead of creating his own poetic speech like Eliot, he returned to the poetic drama of the Elizabethan age. Fry's drama concentrates on characters who are metaphorically lost in a society they do not value and which they feel estranged from. These characters find themselves and their purposes in life through Love – love of God, love of another human being, or love of, acceptance of, themselves.

Terence Rattigan (1911–1977) followed in Ibsen's footsteps in his *The Winslow Boy* (1946) and *The Browning Version* (1948), depicting lives that are destroyed because of deceit and hypocrisy, both on the part of individuals, and on the part of society.

Ibsen and American drama

American drama also reflected Ibsen's influence as it critically examined its own society.

In *All My Sons* (1947) by Arthur Miller (1915–), we see the conflicts between the family and society and, as in Ibsen's *Ghosts* and *The Wild Duck*, how the sins of the parents can be visited upon the children. *Death of a Salesman* (1949) depicts the danger of a life built on a lie, showing how lives can be destroyed if the truth is not found. *The Crucible* (1952) examines the *nature* of a lie. John Proctor is charged by his society because of a lie; when he tells the truth he is accused of lying. The irony of Proctor's situation is that, if he would only co-operate with his society in admitting the 'truth' of that lie, his life would be saved.

Eugene O'Neill's (1888–1953) largely autobiographical *Long Day's Journey into Night* (1940) expounds, in a harrowing and powerful manner, the Ibsenist theory of the sins of the parents being visited upon the children. Each character must travel through his or her own purgatory, from which they emerge, with varying degrees of success, to self-knowledge and a kind of redemption. Past lies have caused personal and social destruction, but O'Neill shows us that the acceptance of truth, and with it an acknowledgement of liability, can bring liberation and peace to those who seek it.

Bertolt Brecht and alienation

During the nineteen thirties and forties, British and American dramatists used the medium of illusionistic theatre to examine the interconnecting strands of society and the pressures they exert on the individual. During the same period, the German, Bertolt Brecht, was striving to demonstrate man's role as an integral part of society by the already mentioned *alienation* theatre.

As we have seen, alienation theatre requires that the audience must not become emotionally involved with a production. It is, however, extremely difficult not to become emotionally involved with Brecht's characters. By virtue of his great skill they are not one-dimensional figures but well-rounded personalities, not ciphers but perfect representations of humanity – weak, selfish, flawed.

Brecht does, however, encourage his audience to form their own conclusions about the purpose of his dramas by ensuring that his plays are open to a multiplicity of interpretations. *Mother Courage and her Children* (1941) is a powerful anti-war play and yet it is a play in which no one actually voices pacifist ideals. Though all detest the war, most desire it too for the advantages it brings. *Galileo* (1939) has truth as a theme, but it can also be read as an examination of the dangers of pursuing science for its own sake rather than as a means of easing human suffering. *The Caucasian Chalk Circle* (1948) can be read as a communist tract, a play about justice, an ironic depiction of hero worship, or a play about love and loyalty.

The influence of French drama: the existential

French audiences have always viewed the theatre not so much as a place of entertainment but as a venue where dramatists would discuss important ideas and depict new issues. Because of this in-built expectation and receptiveness, French dramatists have exercised considerable influence upon their public. While other nations' dramatists were attempting to find a role for man in society during the early years of the twentieth century, so, too, French dramatists searched for a philosophy that would give mankind an identity. For many French dramatists, the answer seemed to lie in the philosophy of *existentialism*.

Existentialist drama portrays a prevailing sense of the pointlessness of all ideals, and the hopelessness of anyone trying to find a sense of purpose in life. Man should not indulge in a wasted search for a God who does not exist. Instead of looking for that God – a search that is only engaged in in order to give life meaning – the individual must look to himself and carve out his own reason for existence.

Jean-Paul Sartre (1905–1980) was a French philosopher, novelist and dramatist who preached the doctrine of existentialism. In plays like *The Flies* (1942) and *In Camera* (1944), hell is shown to be other people – family, friends, society – who, because of the claims they make on the individual, rob him or her of his or her freedom. Sartre's novels and plays all deal with the freeing of the human spirit, a freedom that can only be achieved at the expense of moral values.

Jean Anouilh (1910–1987) was also an existentialist and, in his *Antigone* (1944) and *Becket* (1959), we are shown the conflict between the beliefs of the individual and those of the representative of the State. In both cases the State is stronger than the individual and the individual pays the supreme penalty. Death is the agent that frees these characters' spirits from the clutches of an authoritarian state, but Anouilh makes it plain that death is preferable to denying one's self simply to live.

Samuel Beckett (1906–1989) and Eugene Ionesco (1912–) were also existentialists, but they produced drama that came to be known as the *Theatre of the Absurd*. Theatre of the Absurd dramatists also believe in the senselessness and absurdity of life, but, rather than including reasoned argument in their work, they prefer to simply present that absurdity.

Samuel Beckett, though Irish by birth, wrote many of his plays in French and declared himself an adopted Frenchman. In *Waiting for Godot* (1955) and *Endgame* (1958) Beckett concentrates on man's inner life, representing loss of human control and loss even of human identity – in *Endgame* he reduces two of his characters to dustbins. For Beckett, the ultimate absurdity, the ultimate futility, is mankind desiring an outside agency to control his life. Instead of continually looking for someone or something to give life meaning, mankind must find his own purpose, his own reason for being.

In Ionesco's *Rhinoceros* (1960) all the characters in the play gradually succumb to the highly contagious rhinoceros fever. The fever is a metaphor for conformism – that blind, unthinking desire to believe what the majority in society believes, and to behave as the majority of society behaves so as not to be an outsider. Ionesco had seen people being infected by mob hysteria at large meetings and had been horrified both by their frenzy and by his own feelings of succumbing to it. In the play the central character Béranger fights the disease, but we are given no indication that he will overcome it, i.e., retain his own individuality.

The Theatre of the Absurd has had a wide-ranging influence upon such disparate writers as Stoppard, Pinter and Orton.

British drama of the 1950s and '60s

Osborne, Wesker, Arden, Pinter and Stoppard belong to the generation of playwrights born in the 1930s, who came to the fore in the late 1950s and '60s. These playwrights replaced the middle-class idiom, which had dominated the British stage, with regional and lower-class vernaculars that had rarely been seen on the stage, unless it was to delineate a comic character.

Previously, too, in drama, violence – both physical and verbal – could always be traced to an identifiable cause, and there was usually the suggestion that once the cause had been eradicated all would be well. From the late 1950s onwards, the sources of violence became less clear and less controllable.

Look Back in Anger (1956), by John Osborne (1929–), is commonly referred to as a watershed in British drama. It was the first play to begin the trend away from the middle-class drawing room towards the working-class kitchen, and it introduced the concept of the 'angry young man' to the stage. (Actually, the play's 'hero', Jimmy Porter, was not completely original. Shakespeare's Hamlet striding morosely about the stage, at odds both with himself and his society, is a clear counterpart of what we now call the 'angry young man'.) In *Look Back in Anger*, *The Entertainer* (1957), and *Inadmissible Evidence* (1964) feelings of inadequacy, loneliness and menace predominate, and in the portrayal of explosive anger few dramatists can equal Osborne's skill.

In contrast to Osborne's fiery rhetoric Harold Pinter (1930–) can seem almost clinically detached. In plays like *The Birthday Party* (1958), *The Dumb Waiter* (1960), and *The Caretaker* (1960), Pinter adopted Chekhov's use of oblique dialogue but carried it much further, using sentences that accurately reflect the commonplace trivialities of ordinary speech. Pinter sensed that inarticulate, incoherent speech could be just as dramatic as great eloquence. His dialogue may give us little actual information but its very emptiness gives it great *dramatic* impact.

Arnold Wesker (1932–), conversely, presents everything very clearly. His plays are essentially autobiographical and, like Ibsen and Brecht, he attempts through his work to better the conditions of his fellow human beings. To achieve his aims he uses a relatively straightforward representation of ordinary speech in plays like 'The Wesker Trilogy' (*Chicken Soup with Barley* (1958), *Roots* (1959), and *I'm Talking about Jerusalem* (1960)), and *Chips With Everything* (1962).

For John Arden (1930–) in *Sergeant Musgrave's Dance* (1959), an unusual blend of realism, songs, ballads and verse combine to form the basis of a modern morality play. Here he depicts a soldier sickened by his life and by a society which expects him to carry out its orders even if they are unacceptable to the individual, and yet accepts no shared guilt, no sense of joint responsibility.

Robert Bolt (1924–) and Peter Shaffer (1926–) present interestingly opposing views of mankind in *A Man for All Seasons* (1960) and *The Royal Hunt of the Sun* (1964). Bolt's *A Man for All Seasons* uses a historical background as a backdrop to his examination of the role and place of the individual in an authoritarian society. Bolt's interest lies in the psychology of a man whom we would consider to be a privileged member of society, a man who possesses all that his society can offer, and yet who is prepared to die for a principle. Peter Shaffer in *The Royal Hunt of the Sun* depicts and contrasts an insular, happy, but rigidly controlled society with an outward-looking, class-ridden, and apparently more liberal society. In the central character of Pizarro, we see a man of no principles, devoid of conventional belief, an outcast from society because of his lowly birth, desperately seeking to make sense of his life and to find a reason for it.

Tom Stoppard (1937–) is probably one of the most innovative dramatists of recent years. In *Rosencrantz and Guildenstern are Dead* (1966) and *The Real Inspector Hound* (1968) Stoppard takes the Absurdist doctrine of the loss of human control and marries it to the Brechtian theory of alienation. At all times he wants his audience to realize that they are watching a play, because he wants the audience to concentrate on his main theme of the powerlessness of the individual. Stoppard is fascinated not by the heroes and heroines of life but by the also-rans, the losers. There is humour and there is pathos in his work, and, by constantly shifting reference points, Stoppard has created his own highly individual style of drama.

Summary

Clearly, then, what we refer to as 'modern' drama today is not a group of plays which suddenly and inexplicably appeared on the stage. Twentieth century plays are a product of, and an evolution of, what has gone before. Today's lack of Christian belief has certainly produced dramatists who seek, where previously there was no need, to establish a reason and purpose for mankind's existence. The language modern dramatists use too, which took its inspiration from Strindberg and Chekhov, is more realistic, more akin to ordinary speech. Yet the essential aims of the dramatists remain the same. They seek, as dramatists have always done, to mirror the inner hopes, dreams and fears of mankind.

The fourteen dramatists I have selected for this book were chosen on the basis that their work was representative of the different styles of drama which flourished between 1900 and 1970. O'Casey, Synge, Brighouse and Sherriff may seem to be too early to be termed modern dramatists, but each contributed important elements to the development of more recent drama. Synge and O'Casey broke down the traditional barriers between comedy and tragedy, Brighouse examined the role of women, and Sherriff depicted the horrors of a war that was to alter the shape of society for ever. Similarly, Anouilh's drama, with its roots in existentialism, and Beckett, with his contribution to the Theatre of the Absurd, could not be omitted because of their influence upon such important dramatists as Pinter and Stoppard. Nor would a study of modern drama have been complete without an examination of Miller and Brecht, whose depiction of the role of mankind and society was to be so ably continued by Shaffer, Bolt, Fry and Osborne.

To ensure some standardization, all the dates given for the various plays' first production are those that appear in the *Oxford Companion to English Literature (New Edition)* ed. Margaret Drabble, 1985.

J. M. Synge

John Millington Synge was born near Dublin in 1871 and died in 1909. The son of a barrister, he graduated from Trinity College, Dublin, and then travelled extensively in Europe for many years before settling in Paris for a time. There he met the Irish poet and playwright W. B. Yeats who persuaded him to leave France for the Aran Islands off the coast of Ireland. Yeats had been so impressed by his own visit to the Aran Islands that he wanted Synge to live amongst the people and then to write of his homeland.

Synge's most noted plays are *The Shadow of the Glen* (1903), *Riders to the Sea* (1904), *The Playboy of the Western World* (1907), and *The Tinker's Wedding* (1908).

Synge's plays were, in part, a product of the revival in interest in Irish literature that arose during the last years of the nineteenth century. Many Irish writers of the time were tired of the portrayal of their countrymen as either sentimental buffoons or roaring drunkards, but they were equally unhappy with what Synge himself called the 'joyless' drama of Ibsen.

While Synge acknowledged the necessity for the harsh realism of Ibsen's work, he also argued that the 'real' world held contrasting and complementary moments of joy and laughter — elements he considered absent from Ibsen's drama. This combination of laughter and tragedy is one of the main characteristics of Synge's work.

Synge employs three different types of humour in his drama. The pure humour of ludicrous situations, the ironic humour of ideas, and the sharp, satirical humour he reserved largely for the Roman Catholicism of Western Ireland.

Though Synge had a compassionate view of humanity he did not possess an idealized view of peasant life. Many of his female characters in particular are lonely, prematurely aged, and bitter after their years of toil on the land. Similarly, though he clearly admired the stoical endurance of the peasant classes, this did not blind him to the fact that these same people could be capable of great brutality.

The societies Synge describes are close-knit, insular little worlds. Outside these worlds lies a threatening, alien land of judges, policemen, and soldiers. Despite this fear and distrust of the 'outside', however, there is always the suggestion that the alien land is also a land of greater personal freedom and self-fulfilment.

Synge's peasants speak a dialect that is rich, colourful, and full of allusions to the Bible and Shakespeare. Though it is rather unlikely that any peasant class would voice their opinions and thoughts in quite the grandiose manner Synge envisages, this in no way detracts from the overall impact of his plays.

The Playboy of the Western World

Michael Flaherty and his daughter Pegeen own a country public house in the west of Ireland. Shawn Keogh, Pegeen's cousin and a timid youth, considers himself engaged to Pegeen but, on the arrival of Christy Mahon at the public house, Pegeen transfers her affections to the newcomer. Christy has supposedly murdered his father, but instead of being handed over to the police he finds himself honoured and admired by the local community. Christy's father, however, is not dead, and when he arrives at the inn Christy's admirers desert him. To reinstate himself Christy apparently kills his father but instead of praising him the locals are horrified, fearing they may in some way be implicated. They bind him in order to take him to the nearest police station but, of course, Christy's father isn't really dead. Father and son leave the inn, vowing never to return.

Act 1

Notice how much we learn about Pegeen and her fiancé, Shawn Keogh, from their first conversations.

Shawn is weak and cowardly, refusing to go to the wake because it would mean walking there in the dark. He has left a possibly gravely injured man lying in a ditch near the public house because he was too frightened to go to investigate. His religion is a source of fear rather than comfort to him, for he is continually terrified of doing anything that might arouse the ire and condemnation of Father Reilly, the local priest.

Pegeen, in contrast, has a much more casual attitude to her faith. She mimics the priest without fear and is scathing of Shawn's awe of the Catholic Church. She has no illusions about

Shawn's shortcomings but we feel that she has agreed to marry him, quite simply, because there is no one else. Her temperament is altogether more volatile than Shawn's, as we see clearly in her dealings with her father and his friends.

Notice that it takes Christy almost four pages of dialogue to reveal not only that he has killed his father but *how* he killed his father. Synge perfectly captures the slowness of his peasants' speech, their intense curiosity about the stranger in their midst, their continual probing until they find out what they want to know.

Consider the reactions of the people present in the inn to Christy's revelations of patricide. Michael's friends regard the crime with respect, Pegeen with admiration. When Pegeen suggests that Christy be taken on as pot-boy at the inn, the only person who sees the incongruity of employing a murderer as Pegeen's protector is Shawn, whom everyone despises as a weakling. What do you suppose we are meant to learn from this?

Consider why Pegeen should elevate Christy so quickly into the realms of the romantic hero. Notice how she compares him to the great Irish poets who all possessed violent tempers when angered. Remember how unprepossessing her fiancé is.

Conversely, Widow Quinn is believed to have murdered her husband and yet *her* 'crime' did not win her any glory in the neighbourhood. Examine her 'crime' in comparison to Christy's and see why this should be so.

The verbal fight between Widow Quinn and Pegeen — the older woman and the younger woman pursuing the same man — is a standard feature of this type of comedy. So, too, are Christy's last words in this act when he declares he would have murdered his father sooner if he had known that women would have fought over him because of it. The two incidents, however, do not simply depict humour. Consider the loneliness of the two women and Christy that lies behind these incidents.

Act 2

Remembering that this is a small, isolated community, try to explain why the local girls should be so eager to see a person who has committed what we would consider an appalling crime. Sara decides that Christy is a wonder of the western world. Murder is not normally considered 'a wonder', and the term 'the western world' is one usually reserved for the United States of America. Examine the double irony in Sara's words.

Consider, too, the sharply satirical comment Synge puts into Sara's mouth when, thinking Christy has left, she prepares to take his boots 'for walking to the priest . . . with nothing worth while to confess at all'. Decide whether the satire is aimed at Sara's view of religion, the priest, the religion itself, or all three.

Pegeen takes sadistic pleasure in describing a hanging to Christy because she is jealous of the interest he takes in the other girls. Her words, however, not only reinforce to him that without her protection the same fate would befall him, but also reveal that the highly romantic picture Christy has of her is as false as the one she has of him. Widow Quinn describes Pegeen as a normal peasant girl 'itching and scratching', with 'the stale stink of poteen on her'. Compare this reality with Christy's elevated description of his beloved.

Notice the introduction of pathos in the play when Christy reveals that he welcomed the girls' attention because he was 'born lonesome'. Clearly he has always felt outside of society, felt that he did not belong. Consider how far this background explains why Christy brags so much about his 'murder', and revels in his new found notoriety.

The play is obviously being built on a series of lies and self-deceptions. Christy, we discover, did not kill his father, but he is only accepted by the community and Pegeen on the understanding that he did commit the deed. Christy loves a Pegeen who is altogether gentler and finer in his imagination than she is in fact. Pegeen loves a Christy who, according to his father, is a total fraud.

Act 3

Compare old Mahon's description of the Christy he knew – a man who was the butt of every joke, reviled and abused by everyone – and the Christy who is the hero of the hour. If we accept that what old Mahon says about his son is the truth, why is he so different now? Remember that previously he was lonely and now he is loved, before he was abused and now he is honoured, at home he was isolated and now he is a person of consequence.

When Christy asks Pegeen to marry him she accepts. For

Pegeen, Christy is a fairy-tale hero suddenly transformed into a flesh and blood man, but the fairy tale comes to an abrupt end when old Mahon appears. Not unreasonably Christy points out that he is still the same man who wooed and won her but Pegeen will not be placated. Consider why this should be so.

Notice that Christy is so desperate for Pegeen's love that he attacks and apparently kills his father. He is convinced that she will admire and love him once more. Ironically, it is Pegeen who organizes the menfolk to bind him and Pegeen who burns his leg when he struggles. Christy's unverified, romantic tale of murder is acceptable, the reality occurring before your very eyes is not.

Consider how the experiences of the past few days have changed Christy. He is no longer afraid of his father and agrees to go with him only if his father consents to be his servant. He has a new confidence and strength and, recognizing the change in himself, he ironically thanks the assembled crowd for their part in his transformation. He has lost his innocent naïvety, and we sense that he will be the manipulator in the future, not the manipulated.

For Pegeen the end of the play also brings the end of her dream and the end of the reality. Having found her fairy-tale hero and, in a way, made him into what he now is — a truly strong, fearless man — she has not only lost him but also lost the illusion she cherished.

Assignments

1 Discuss how the mixture of comedy and pathos adds to the play's impact. Look for contrasting moments of humour and sadness. Christy's bragging is humorous, but it is also sad to think he has to pretend to be what he is not, in order to be accepted. Pegeen creates a make-believe hero out of a very ordinary Christy, but consider the loneliness, the dreams, that must lie behind the necessity to do such a thing. At the end of the play all her hopes and fantasies come to nothing and she is left alone. Look at Shawn. He appears a pathetic weakling. Consider, however, why he should always be so afraid. Look at his religion. Even his undoubted love for Pegeen is tinged with fear of his quite natural physical desire for her. Look, too, at the Widow Quinn. Examine the other characters' reactions to her. Is she a figure of fun, of tragedy, or both?

2 Compare and contrast the characters of Christy and Shawn.

3 Consider the importance of the Widow Quinn and old Mahon to the plot.

4 Write a short story depicting what you think might happen to Christy and his father after they leave Flaherty's public house. Perhaps they could emigrate to America and make their fortune there, or perhaps they could leave for Dublin and buy their own public house. What kind of man do you think Christy will be after his experiences? Include any changes you imagine might happen to his character in your short story.

Harold Brighouse

Harold Brighouse was born in Eccles, Lancashire in 1882. On leaving school he worked for a time in a textile export business. At the age of twenty he moved to London to work and became fired with enthusiasm for the theatre. From 1909 onwards he earned his living as a writer, writing fifteen full-length plays, over fifty one-act plays, and eight novels before his death in 1958.

Brighouse was one of the most successful of what is referred to as the Manchester School of Dramatists. At the beginning of the twentieth century a Miss A. E. Horniman provided funds to found repertory theatres in Dublin, Manchester and Liverpool in an attempt to encourage local dramatists to write plays set in their own environments. *Hobson's Choice*, which was produced first in America in 1915 and then in London in 1916, has remained one of the most enduringly popular examples of the Manchester School of Dramatists.

Hobson's Choice

The plot is basically that of a modern fairy-tale – the poor 'nobody' who falls in love with the 'princess' and finds riches. The play concerns a shy and somewhat backward boot-maker, Willie Mossop, who marries – rather against his will – his boss Henry Hobson's efficient and determined daughter Maggie. Under Maggie's influence Willie grows in confidence and authority and eventually takes over Hobson's business, becoming not only a man of note in the community but also a fitting and loving husband for Maggie.

Act 1

We are introduced to the three Hobson daughters – Alice, Vickey and Maggie. Alice is knitting, Vickey is reading and Maggie is doing the accounts. Neither Alice nor Vickey know if their father has had his breakfast yet, and have to ask Maggie. Consider how much we learn from this apparently unimportant information about the characters of the girls.

In a comedy the follies and foibles of characters are exposed for us to laugh at, but in order to achieve this successfully there has to be at least one character who serves as a yardstick for us to judge those other characters by. In *Hobson's Choice* this character is Maggie. Through her words and what is said to her, for example, we see very quickly how shallow and pretentious her sisters are, and how weak Freddy and Albert are.

Henry Hobson is a pompous bully who likes to think that he is master in his own home, but we quickly realize that it is Maggie who does all the work, Maggie who is in control. Indeed, one of the themes of the play is the right of women to control their own destinies – a right Hobson is vehemently against. *He* will decide what his daughters wear, *he* will choose Alice and Vickey's husbands. There will be no husband, of course, for Maggie, because he considers her too old at thirty to marry. The real reason is his selfish awareness that he could not run the business without her.

Notice how ingeniously Brighouse introduces the play's highly unlikely hero, Willie Mossop. When Mrs Hepworth asks to see who made the boots she ordered, we learn not only that Willie, for all his unprepossessing appearance and apparent lack of intelligence, has a real talent for making boots, but also the conditions he works in as he climbs up into the daylight from the cellar.

Examine the paradox of the reversal of the conventional marriage proposal. It is Maggie who asks the somewhat slow-witted Willie to marry her and not Willie who asks her. Maggie is not a bit daunted when Willie declares bluntly that he doesn't love her and has an 'understanding' with Ada Figgins, his landlady's daughter. Consider Maggie's judgement of that possible match. Ada, she points out, is helpless and clinging. Married to her, Willie will remain where he is in society – an underpaid bootmaker in 'Hobson's'. If Willie marries Maggie, however, she vows that she will make him a success in the world. Notice that Maggie never for one moment deliberates as to whether she or Ada would make Willie the *happier*. Notice, too, how weak Willie appears. When Maggie vanquishes Ada he hardly says a word, other than to worry about what will happen when he returns to his lodgings that night and has to meet the formidable Mrs Figgins. As soon as Maggie says he will never have to return to his lodgings ever again, he seems quite content to have her manage his life.

Consider why Alice and Vickey are so horrified by Maggie's proposed marriage. They are not concerned with whether their sister will be happy with Willie or not, but what the repercussions may be on their social status if they have a boot-maker as a brother-in-law.

Notice that Maggie gives her father the opportunity to employ both herself and Willie after their marriage. She does not want to undermine the shop by taking away its best asset – Willie's skill. Hobson, however, being a bully at heart, thinks to physically beat the idea of marriage out of Willie's mind. Hobson hits Willie only once and we see our 'hero's' first sign of independence. He does not *love* Maggie. His kiss cements his and Maggie's engagement, but it is not a kiss of love. The kiss is a kiss of defiance.

Act 2

Notice how little Alice and Vickey still know about the business that feeds and clothes them, and that they are unable to do something as simple as counting correctly. Tubby, the elderly shoemaker, realizes that 'Hobson's' cannot survive long with Willie gone, but Alice and Vickey care nothing for the business. They care only that when Maggie marries Willie, hopes of grand marriages for themselves may be blighted.

Consider how grudgingly Alice and Vickey agree to attend Maggie's wedding, and how horrified they are at Maggie's commonsense attitude of wanting a brass ring from the shop to use as a wedding ring. What kind of impression do you think we are to have of the three sisters and their values, when Maggie wants to clear out the attic to furnish her new home? Initially, Alice and Vickey are appalled at this, and vow that they would never begin their marriages with second-hand furniture, but examine how their views alter when they see the broken chairs their sister is taking away.

Act 3

We are beginning to measure the other men in the play against the character of Willie. This is ironic and meant to be so. Willie is the least educated, the least successful, and the least valued of the men we encounter in the play. Yet, when Freddy and Albert laugh at Willie we are as angry as Maggie is. Society's values are shown to be false in comparison to Willie's essential goodness of heart.

Notice that Hobson comes to Maggie when he is in distress. Notice, too, that he fears social disgrace more than financial ruin. What does this tell us of the town they live in, the society they are part of? He vows that he was only drunk at twelve o'clock in the morning because he was attempting to 'forget that I'd a thankless child' – a humorous echo of the words spoken by Shakespeare's King Lear. When Albert declares that if Hobson wishes to keep his name out of the newspapers he must settle out of court for the sum of £1000, notice that it is Maggie who declares that her father can only afford £500. We know that this money will be shared equally between her sisters as their wedding settlements. Remembering how Maggie's father and sisters have treated her, explain what this incident reveals to us about her character.

Brighouse beautifully reveals that his efficient, determined, calculating heroine has a sensitive soul. Maggie retains one of Mrs Hepworth's flowers to press as a keepsake of her wedding day. Consider why she should be so embarrassed when Willie sees her keeping the flower. Remember he has told her he does not love her. Remember, too, the years she has endured trying to keep the business afloat, and that all she has ever received is resentment. Consider how her society viewed her before her marriage – the stock old maid, a figure of ridicule and amusement.

Act 4

Concerned about his master's health, Tubby has brought Maggie back to 'Hobson's'. When she arrives, Hobson's doctor asks if she is prepared to return home to take care of her father. To Hobson's disbelief – and ours – Maggie states firmly that she must ask her husband's opinion before she can make any decision.

Notice the continuation of the echo from *King Lear* when Hobson asks his three daughters in turn to come home to look after him. Ironically, King Lear and Hobson *are* alike. Both of them are tyrants, both are abused and deceived by two of their three daughters and only truly loved by one. What makes the comparison so amusing is that Lear has the stature and majesty of a figure of supreme tragedy, whereas Hobson is merely a petty, blustering despot.

Notice that while neither Alice nor Vickey is willing to leave their new homes, their primary concern is the possibility that if Maggie returns home she may persuade their father to make a will leaving nothing to them. Brighouse does not condemn the two sisters for their grasping natures, nor does he have his central character Maggie attack them. He allows Vickey and Alice to condemn themselves out of their own mouths.

Consider how much more confident and assured Willie has become. He scathingly refuses the offer Hobson makes to him to come back to the shop on his old wages, declaring that he and his wife will only return to 'Hobson's' on *his* terms. He even over-rides Maggie's objections about the name that must appear over the shop. Explain what has brought about this transformation in him.

The fairy-tale has ended as it should. The villain, Hobson, has been deflated. His victim – Willie – who has been abused and exploited for years is now a triumphant hero, but his nature has not changed. He does not revel in his success over his former employer but has sympathy for him. Willie has defied Maggie, too, over the question of the shop name, and she is proud of his independence. Maggie no longer dominates her weak husband, but neither will Willie dominate her. Their marriage is now truly a partnership – a business partnership and a loving partnership. Our heroine now has a fitting hero.

Assignments

1 **In drama, even up to the present day, women have tended to be portrayed as subservient and inferior to men. Discuss the role of women in the play.**

Suggestions for your answer:
Look at Alice and Vickey's interests and values. How does Brighouse reveal that he considers them to be shallow and false? Remember that the audience would see Alice and Vickey as 'normal' middle-class women. Women of the time were not supposed to work or be involved in business. Why, therefore, does the audience not see Maggie as unfeminine or too

revolutionary? Consider Maggie and the attitudes of the other characters in the play to her. She manages the shop single-handedly, but examine her relationship with her father. Look at what he allows her to do and what he forbids her to do – are there contradictions? What do Alice and Vickey think of their sister? Do they envy her her mental ability? Look at Albert's encounter with Maggie in the shop when she sells him the boots. What kind of impression does Brighouse intend us to have of his heroine from this incident? What do Freddy and Albert think of Maggie? Examine their conversations with Willie after his marriage to Maggie. Notice that Maggie does not become subservient to Willie when he becomes strong and independent. Why not?

2 Hobson is a pompous, overbearing bully. Does he have any redeeming features?

3 Write an additional scene for the play to be inserted at the end of Act 3. In this scene Vickey and Alice discuss Maggie, her new husband Willie, and their shop in Oldfield Road. Remember how opposed they were to the marriage, how snobbish they are. They might comment on the wedding itself and compare it to the weddings they plan to have. Try to capture the flavour of the characters that Brighouse portrays.

Sean O'Casey

Sean O'Casey was born in Dublin in 1880, the youngest of thirteen children. After a childhood cruelly blighted by malnutrition and deprivation, he worked as a general labourer, teaching himself to read and write. His creative talent was recognized by Lady Gregory, one of the founders of the Abbey Theatre in Dublin, and in 1923 his play *The Shadow of the Gunman* received favourable critical notices. *Juno and the Paycock* (1924) reinforced his reputation as one of the foremost dramatists of his day, but *The Plough and the Stars* (1926) caused a riot in the theatre because of O'Casey's somewhat ironical treatment of the Easter Rising of 1916. O'Casey left Ireland for England, but continued to write for the stage, notably in *The Silver Tassie* (1928), *Purple Dust* (1940), *Cock-a-Doodle Dandy* (1949) and *The Bishop's Bonfire* (1955). He died in 1964.

Though O'Casey's drama portrays the political themes of his time his characters are in no sense mere cyphers or mouthpieces for his views. His portraits of ordinary Irish people trying desperately to exist amongst the wreckage of their homes have the ring of absolute truth. Characters like Juno, Bessie Burgess and Fluther Good live and breathe with a vibrancy that is impressive.

O'Casey's language is rich and fluid, accurately depicting the Irish idiom and conveying with great power and intensity the despair, tragedy, sparkling humour and ironic wit of his people.

Juno and the Paycock

The events of the play take place during the civil war between the newly created Free State and the Republicans in 1922, when Irishmen fought one another for supremacy in the land.

Captain Boyle (the 'paycock' or peacock of the title), his wife Juno, daughter Mary and crippled son Johnny live in a Dublin tenement surviving largely because of Juno's resilience and endeavour. The Boyles believe that at last their lives have changed for the better when they learn from Charles Bentham, the schoolmaster, that one of their relatives, a Mr Ellison, has died leaving money to be shared equally between Captain Boyle and his cousin Michael Finnegan.

On the strength of this inheritance the family get themselves even deeper into debt and Mary rejects her socialist suitor Jerry Devine in favour of the middle-class Charles Bentham. The Boyles' good fortune does not last. Bentham, who drew up the will, failed to name Captain Boyle and his cousin Michael Finnegan as the beneficiaries, but wrote instead that the inheritance was to be shared between Mr Ellison's first and second cousins. There are so many first and second cousins that there is no money left.

Mary is pregnant by Bentham, who has left Ireland for England never to return. Johnny is executed by his former Republican compatriots because he informed on one of their members. Juno's despair is complete. She leaves her husband and goes with her daughter to try and make a new life for the two of them and the unborn child.

Act 1

Examine the description we are given of Juno Boyle. In her youth she was a pretty woman but years of struggle have left their mark on her. She harangues her husband with a biting, sarcastic humour, but we sense that she speaks more out of habit and to keep herself sane than with any belief that her words will change him. Notice, too, how cynical she is about her daughter Mary being on strike because of a principle. People in their social position, she declares, cannot afford the luxury of 'principles'.

Mary reads Ibsen – in particular *The Doll's House*, *The Wild Duck* and *Ghosts*. *The Doll's House* has as one of its themes the heroine's feeling of being enmeshed and crushed by the society she lives in. In *The Wild Duck* the father Hjalmar is lazy, self-centred, and lives on the dream of producing an important invention, a dream that never materializes. In *Ghosts* past events resurface to destroy the present happiness of the central characters. Notice the similarity between *The Doll's House* and *The Wild Duck* and Mary's present situation. She, too, feels at odds with her society and wants something better. Her father, like Hjalmar, is a shiftless, selfish dreamer. We know immediately that Mary's dreams will come to nothing. Some occurrence from the past will blight her hopes.

Consider O'Casey's view of trade unionism through his portrayal of Jerry Devine. Devine, he declares, is a man who knows only enough to incite his powerful union into action but not enough to see that the power of his men could be used to help mankind.

Look at the character of Captain Boyle. He has a list of fictitious ailments which manifest themselves whenever an offer of work appears. Despite his declaration that he sailed from Mexico to the Antarctic Ocean, his title of 'Captain' is a fraud. He was only once at sea in a coal ship from Dublin to Liverpool, and then he was seasick the entire time. Clearly he is a lazy scoundrel and yet he also possesses an undoubted charm.

Joxer is by turns Boyle's best friend and his worst enemy, depending upon whether Boyle has the money for some drinks or not. He is shifty, cringing, and an expedient liar whose views change according to the company he is with. Initially, he appears to have no opinions of his own, but we quickly realize that this is a deliberate policy, because only by being all things to all men can he survive in the way that he wants to.

Compare Joxer's easy-going attitude to that of Charles Bentham. Bentham is a schoolmaster not a lawyer, but his personal pride blinds him to the possibility that he does not have the expertise to draft a will properly. This pride will have catastrophic results for the Boyles. Notice how determinedly jovial he appears in the Boyles' flat. He is uncomfortable with them and tries too hard to pretend that he is not.

Humorous incidents abound in Act 1. We see Juno pretending to have left the flat so that she can spring out on the unsuspecting Joxer and her husband like some goddess of retribution, and Boyle loathing his relation Mr Ellison, but plunging his entire family into mourning when he hears of the inheritance. Mingled with this humour, however, we have the figure of Johnny, the Boyles' only son, who is shattered in body and mind.

Act 2

Consider the difference in Captain Boyle's opinion of the clergy in this act with what it was in Act 1. Why has he changed his view? Remember that wealth brings with it status, a new position in society. Boyle is a vain man. Will he want to stand against the establishment view of the clergy?

Unlike the Boyles, who are Catholic, Bentham declares himself to be a theosophist, a follower of an Eastern philosophy which states that man's happiness depends upon his sympathy with the Universal spirit. Notice not only how much more simple and sincerely felt Juno's beliefs are, but consider, too, whether Bentham *really* believes the philosophy, or whether he holds it simply because it sets him apart.

Examine how O'Casey personalizes the political differences between the Irish Free Staters and the Republicans when Robbie Tancred is killed. The opposing dogmas are irrelevant. All we see is the grief of a mother for her dead son.

Notice, too, that immediately after Mrs Tancred's most moving prayer, O'Casey reinforces the cruel fact that grief is purely personal. Despite the fact that there has been a death in the house the Boyles put on a merry gramophone record. Then, when they see Robbie Tancred's hearse is departing for the cemetery, they go outside to watch the event with the disinterested curiosity of spectators. It is not that they are uncaring or unfeeling, it is just that Robbie's death does not touch them personally.

Act 3

Disaster comes fast and furious towards the Boyle family. We learn that Captain Boyle had apparently known for some time that he would receive nothing from Ellison's will. Consider why he should have allowed his family to go deeper and deeper into debt. Remember that before the acquisition of his supposed wealth he was the subject of amusement and derision in the community.

Examine the family's reaction to Mary's pregnancy. Boyle considers the social disgrace and declares that he will throw his daughter out of the house. Johnny says that Mary should be driven from the door. Only Juno feels pity for her daughter, and vows that if Mary has to leave the house she will go with her. Knowing what we do of Boyle and Johnny's characters, consider how justified their reactions are to Mary's pregnancy.

Look now at Jerry Devine's attitude towards the news of Mary's condition. He used to be her boyfriend and has always prided himself upon his humanity. His charity and understanding, however, do not extend to Mary. Decide whether you feel that Jerry has more justification for his behaviour towards Mary than Bentham, or whether both fail her equally.

Notice how effectively O'Casey uses grim irony to depict Johnny being taken away to be shot, while Juno and Mary are vainly attempting to prevent all their furniture being repossessed. Why should this scene appear more moving because it is presented in this manner, than if Johnny had been 'arrested' while the family still believed themselves rich?

Consider how Joxer and Boyle's drunken, incoherent comments add to, and intensify, both the tragedy and the considerable heroism of Juno, for we know instinctively that despite what she has endured she will survive.

Assignments

1 The title of the play is *Juno and the Paycock*. How much of the impact of the drama depends upon the relationship between Juno and Captain Boyle, and how much is due to other elements?

Suggestions for your answer:
Examine Juno and her husband's conversations, and the comments they make about each other to other characters. Does Juno ever clearly condemn the Captain and his way of life? What kind of relationship does the Captain have with his wife? Are we supposed to see the couple simply as individuals, or does O'Casey intend them to represent a particular type or class in society? Notice how Juno's apparently humorous words hide a life of debt, worry, and grief. She cares so much and yet her husband appears to care not at all. What is the significance in having two characters with such clearly opposing values? Examine, too, the other facets of the play. We know, through the characters of Johnny and Mrs Tancred, that a civil war is raging. How important is this element to the drama? If Mary and her pregnancy were cut from the play, would the loss to the play's impact be great or hardly noticeable?

2 Examine the characters of Jerry Devine and Charles Bentham and explain what you feel they are meant to represent in the play.

3 Captain Boyle is a lazy scoundrel but he also has a certain charm. Explain how you think O'Casey manages to convey these two sides to his character.

4 Imagine that, like the Boyles, you believe that you have been left a large amount of money. What would you spend it on, and what would your feelings be when you discover that it has all been a dreadful mistake and you will receive no money at all? Write a short story in which you describe what happens to you. (Note that your story should *not* simply be a long list of what you might buy.)

R. C. Sherriff

Robert Cedric Sherriff was born in 1896 and educated at Kingston Grammar School and Oxford University. He worked for a time in his father's insurance business, but when the First World War broke out in 1914 he joined the Army. At the end of the war he returned to the family business, but an interest in amateur theatricals persuaded him to begin writing. *Journey's End* was rejected by many theatre companies before the Incorporated Stage Society put on one performance in 1928, and in 1929 the play was finally produced in London.

Sherriff's other noted plays are *Badger's Green* (1930), *Miss Mabel* (1948) and *Home at Seven* (1950). In later life Sherriff wrote screen plays for such films as *The Invisible Man* (1933), *Goodbye Mr Chips* (1933), *No Highway* (1950) and *The Dambusters* (1955). He died in 1975.

Sherriff's drama concentrates on the plight of the individual who is held and controlled by circumstances beyond his control. His heroes and heroines possess a nobility of spirit, but the societies they inhabit value that quality only because it makes them easier to manipulate and control.

Journey's End

The action covers a period of four days during the last months of the First World War. Stanhope, Osborne, Hibbert, Trotter and Raleigh, officers in the British Army, defend a small stretch of land from their dug-out, and wait for what is expected to be a decisive German attack. Raleigh and Osborne are sent with ten men on an ill-conceived and clearly doomed mission to capture some German soldiers for interrogation purposes. Osborne and six of the men are killed, and the single German boy soldier Raleigh captures reveals information that is trivial compared with the value of those killed. The expected German attack begins and we are left at the end of the play with the impression that none of the British officers has survived.

Act 1

Into the close-knit world of the dug-out comes the idealistic, eighteen-year-old Raleigh. Raleigh and Stanhope were at the same school, and Raleigh plainly hero-worshipped the older man. Notice that Raleigh enlisted after Stanhope had visited the school, resplendent in his uniform and wearing his Military Cross. Consider, too, that while no one in the play actually voices the opinion that the war is a futile waste of human life, all the officers prefer youngsters to be sent to the Front. They, alone, still believe that what they are engaged on is a chivalric exercise.

Our preconceptions about life at the Front are shattered along with Raleigh's. We, like him, assume that there will be continuous noise and fighting. The reality is an unnerving silence, cutlets of dubious origin, vague liquids that may be soup or tea, and the crushing disappointment when tins of pineapple turn out to be apricots instead. Small incidents assume an importance far beyond what is merited in the claustrophobic atmosphere – notice Stanhope's reaction to Mason's having forgotten to pack the pepper.

A cynical and ironic sense of humour dominates the men's conversations. Hardy, the previous company commander, reveals that his last officer succumbed to lumbago on his first night in the trenches, and is now employed in Britain lecturing to young officers about life at the front line. When Osborne wishes that they knew more about what was happening, Trotter reveals that, as his wife reads the newspapers every day, he will ask her as she is sure to know. Remember that these men are daily facing possible death. One would think that humour would be the very last emotion to surface in such conditions. Consider why the men's conversations should be so full of amusing reflections.

Notice how Sherriff influences our attitude towards Hibbert by systematically destroying the illusion of Stanhope as the model British soldier. Initially we are inclined to despise Hibbert as all the other men apparently do, because he is always inventing illnesses in the hope that he will be invalided back to Britain. Conversely, we see Stanhope – for all his excessive drinking – as a 'hero'. He is the company commander, he was decorated for bravery, he holds the company together. Gradually, however, we discover that Stanhope is permanently drunk because, if he

33

weren't, he would be so consumed with fear that he couldn't function. At one point he even considered pretending to be ill so that he could be sent home. He didn't actually do it – he decided that it would be a dishonourable thing to do – but he did consider the possibility. He wouldn't go home on his last leave because he couldn't bear Raleigh's sister to see him for what he really is – a terrified drunk. Stanhope is not a 'hero' but neither is Hibbert a coward. They are just two, normal, terrified men.

Act 2 Scene 1

Notice how much of the men's conversations is taken up with reminiscences of their lives at home and yet, ironically, Osborne reveals that when they do go home they can't escape the war. Consider why Osborne should view with such cynicism his children wanting him to help them to arrange a tin-soldier battle.

Look at how sceptical Raleigh already is about the propaganda he, and the people back home, were told about the Germans. Remember that he has only been at the Front for twelve hours.

The only officer who appears to be unaffected by their conditions is Trotter. Trotter appears to be a stereotype of the cheerful, doggedly determined, unimaginative British soldier. Unlike his fellow officers he is plainly working class – notice Sherriff's deliberate dropping of the letter 'h' from Trotter's dialogue to indicate this. Stanhope and Osborne wish they were more like him. They believe that he is more able to bear the war because he has no imagination. Examine Trotter's words and judge whether their assessment of him is an accurate one. Consider the gas attack incident.

Stanhope feels that he is becoming more and more isolated from the rest of humanity, a feeling that terrifies him. Remember that Stanhope's father is a vicar, and yet we see no references to God, or to the comforting possibility of a life after death in Stanhope's conversations. Stanhope has plainly lost his faith, so his sense of isolation may be due to his realization that he is alone in the vastness of the universe.

Examine the incident that occurs when Raleigh wishes to send a letter home. Clearly Stanhope believed that Raleigh would write unflatteringly about him, and that is why he wished to censor the boy's mail. Consider why Raleigh should write nothing but praise about Stanhope. Does he not want to hurt his family by telling them the truth, does he not see – or possibly not want to see – what Stanhope has become? Consider, too, how Stanhope must feel after this incident. He has completely lost his self-control in front of a boy who used to look up to him.

Act 2 Scene 2

Notice that when Stanhope informs his sergeant-major that a massive German attack is expected in two days, both he and the sergeant-major are well aware of the likely outcome of such an attack. Neither of them, however, states the obvious – that they will probably all be killed. Similarly, when the Colonel tells Stanhope that two of his officers and ten of his men are to be sent on what is, in effect, a suicide raid, Stanhope does not question the decision. Consider why, when Stanhope is fully aware of the stupidity of the plan, he remains silent. Is his loyalty and obedience to authority so absolute that he cannot question?

Compare this incident with what happens when Hibbert tells Stanhope that he can bear no more and is going to leave. Notice the comment Stanhope makes about Hibbert's proposed 'accidental' death – 'it often happens out here'. Notice, too, that Hibbert shows a kind of courage when he quietly waits for Stanhope to shoot him, saying he would prefer death now than to go back to the trenches. Stanhope declares, however, that if everyone refused to fight now, it would be an act of disloyalty to those who have already died. To remain where they are is the only thing 'a decent man' can do. Given the difference in language – Stanhope speaks as an Edwardian, public-school-educated man of the time would – are the values he and his men cherish understandable today?

Act 3 Scene 1

The time for the proposed raid on the German line has been altered to dusk, making it even more hazardous, but consider how the Colonel's primary concern is for the safety of the German prisoners they hope to capture. The British soldiers are expendable.

Examine the long conversation Osborne has with Raleigh about the beauties of the English countryside, archaeological digs, and the special meal they are to have when they return from their raid. Consider why, just before their highly dangerous mission, Osborne and Raleigh should talk about such apparently unrelated matters.

When Osborne and six of his men are killed, why should it be ironic that Raleigh only manages to capture one German boy soldier? Look, too, at Stanhope's sarcastic repetition of the words 'How awfully nice – if the brigadier's pleased', the calm way he describes how many of his men were killed, and his ironic question to the Colonel, 'Did you expect them to be all safely back?' Stanhope does not harangue the Colonel, or break down at the waste of human life, but we know how distraught and furious he is. Consider how Sherriff's clever use of apparently innocent dialogue achieves this effect.

Act 3 Scene 2

Examine how Trotter, Hibbert and Stanhope behave, despite the fact that so many of their friends have been killed. Raleigh doesn't join them, he cannot bear to. Can you understand Stanhope's view that they have to pretend that life is going on as it did before or they could not remain sane?

Act 3 Scene 3

Notice that Raleigh likens his fatal injury to one he received while playing rugby at school. Consider what his words tell us about him. He is so young, his only experience of life has been his schooldays, he cannot envisage that his life is over.

Does the fact that the end of the play is deliberately vague about the fates of the other men add to, or detract from, the play's impact?

Assignments

1 Consider how Sherriff depicts not only the horror of war, but also the nobility of the men involved in it.

Suggestions for your answer:
The Colonel sends men on a doomed mission, but it is a mission they go on willingly. Men are shot for desertion when they are, in reality, consumed with fear. Look at the conditions the men

live in, but notice how they make light of their deprivation. Look, too, at the youth and inexperience of the men at the Front – Stanhope is a company commander and yet he is only twenty-one and can have had no experience of war as he came to the Front straight from school. Do you feel that those in authority – i.e. the Colonel, the Brigadier – really understand 'modern' warfare? Look at the various plans they make for the attack on the German line. Does Sherriff intend us to see men like Stanhope, Raleigh, and Osborne as foolish or naïve in their unswerving loyalty to authority, or are we to regard their self-sacrifice as admirable?

2 Write a character study of Raleigh, or, imagining that you are Raleigh, keep a diary of events up to the day of your death.

3 Are the values and opinions expressed in the play relevant to today?

4 Write a scene which you feel would serve as an alternative ending to the play. Perhaps Hibbert could perform an act of outstanding bravery, or Trotter might be the only officer to survive and he could tell us what he *really* thinks. If Stanhope was the only man to survive, how would he cope with the situation?

Bertolt Brecht

Bertolt Brecht was born in Augsburg in what was then the Kingdom of Bavaria in 1898. He left Germany in 1933 on the rise to power of the Nazis and lived in exile in Europe, Scandinavia and America before moving to East Berlin in 1948 where he remained until his death in 1956.

His most noted works are *The Good Woman of Setzuan* (1938–41), *The Life of Galileo* (1939), *Mother Courage and her Children* (1941) and *The Caucasian Chalk Circle* (1948).

Brecht's drama is best known for its probing into moral and social problems. As a communist Brecht professed to hold no Christian beliefs and could be very outspoken in his condemnation of all forms of religion. Despite this, however, he returned again and again in his plays to an examination of virtue and morality as though trying to make sense of them. In *The Good Woman of Setzuan*, for example, Shan Te is made to see that to survive in her society she must temper her goodness with ruthlessness. Galileo in *The Life of Galileo* is a coward not a martyred saint, but he could not have been so creative if his cowardice had not made him cling so tenaciously to life. Mother Courage's children die because they possess the admirable virtues of honesty, bravery, and love, while she – the calculating opportunist – survives. Grusha in *The Caucasian Chalk Circle* displays loyalty, courage, and self-sacrifice and yet the audience has a secret admiration for the cowardly, corrupt Azdak.

Though a communist Brecht was much too deeply concerned with the rights and needs of the individual to be a very successful advocate of communism. None of his plays show the realities of life in a Soviet dominated part of the world and, indeed, all his plays are set in the past not his present. Most of his characters, too, are people who pay lip service to authority, appearing to agree with the laws of that authority, but only so that they are able to survive.

Brecht's theory of alienation (see pp. 2–3) has had a tremendous influence upon several modern dramatists. In many ways it is not a comfortable, nor an easy, drama. Not only must the audience judge, assess, and draw their own conclusions about what they see, but what the audience learns about their own and society's values in the process can be anything but palatable or pleasant to discover.

Mother Courage and her Children

The play concerns the experiences of a woman canteen-owner, Anna Fierling, and her three children, Eilif, Swiss Cheese and Kattrin, during the Thirty Years War, a European war which raged over almost all of Germany from 1618 to 1648.

Anna Fierling, or Mother Courage as she is called by the soldiers, makes a living selling food, drink and equipment to the opposing forces. During the course of the play, she flirts with the cook, looks after an inept chaplain, loses her three children, and is finally left alone at the end of the play while the war rages on.

On one level the play can be read as a powerfully ironic anti-war drama. Sieges do not have 'winners' and 'losers' – everyone suffers because everyone is hungry. The chaplain declares that the war they are fighting is a religious one, but the cook demands to know how anyone can possibly tell the difference. All wars mean death, bribery, plunder and destruction. The soldiers comment that in peace time countries and their peoples become weak and selfish, whereas in war the virtues of order, efficiency and comradeship flourish. Examine both the truth and the irony in these apparent contradictions. Look, too, at the circumstances surrounding Eilif's execution. Why should his death be doubly ironic? Remember that he was previously praised for his bravery, and notice, too, that the country is still at war, though poor communications mean a delay in everyone finding that out.

On another level the play can be seen as a vehicle for Brecht's examination of the nature of morality.

Mother Courage warns Eilif, Swiss Cheese and Kattrin to beware of traits we would consider admirable – the traits of bravery, honesty and love. There is no irony intended in her warning, but *we* can see the irony in the fact that she considers the possession of virtues to be dangerous. Is her view in any sense justified by what happens in the play?

Examine the cook's song in Scene 9. Notice that all the characters he sings about were destroyed because of the virtues they possessed. Solomon was unhappy because he was too wise, Julius Caesar died because he was too brave, Socrates died because he was too honest, and St Martin died because he was too charitable. Those who possess virtues in our society, the cook declares, are crushed by that society. Conversely, those who have no virtue survive and prosper. It is a pessimistic view of humanity, but consider whether it may be a realistic one.

On yet another level, the play can also be read as a portrayal of someone who initially appears to be completely amoral – Mother Courage.

Consider how Mother Courage earned her nickname. She drove through a bombardment, not because she was brave, but because she had fifty loaves that would have been inedible if she had remained where she was.

She refuses to buy bullets from the ordnance officer, not through any sense of morality, not because it would mean men having to go into battle unarmed, but because the price is too high.

She will not give her officers' shirts for bandages, as the peasants who are hurt have no money to pay for them. Her action seems cruelly callous, but think whether there are any extenuating circumstances for her refusal to help. The shirts are part of her stock, part of her income for herself and her dumb daughter Kattrin. If Mother Courage gives the shirts away she will make no money to buy food, but, if she keeps them, the peasants could bleed to death.

When Swiss Cheese is arrested, Mother Courage knows she can save him from death if she bribes the Sergeant. Look at how unflatteringly Mother Courage is portrayed here as she haggles over the price of the wagon. She only decides finally to sell it when she appears to have no other choice. Consider, too, how pitiless and unmaternal she appears when Swiss Cheese's body is shown to her by the soldiers, in the hope she will incriminate herself by identifying him. She denies that he is in any way related to her, denies that she has even seen him before. Can you excuse her behaviour at all?

Examine Scene 4. Mother Courage and a soldier are waiting to make their complaints to the Captain. Mother Courage's grievance is that soldiers have ruined some of her goods, while the soldier wants his reward for saving the Colonel's horse. In the end neither of them waits to see the Captain. Initially, the scene can appear unnecessary, but Brecht is declaring here that the majority of 'ordinary' people – you and I – will not stand up to authority, even though we may know we are in the right. Like Mother Courage and the soldier, we may bluster indignantly about our rights, but we don't stand by our principles. We prefer to avoid confrontation, prefer to inwardly complain, rather than demand what is fair and just. It is a cynical point of view, but consider whether there is any truth in it.

Examine Scene 9 where the cook asks Mother Courage to come with him to open an inn. The inn cannot support three people and the cook does not want Kattrin with them anyway, because she is too disfigured to make an attractive waitress. Given what we have learned of Mother Courage's character, are you surprised when she refuses the cook's offer? The inn is an attractive proposition, it would give her money and security. Mother Courage tells Kattrin later that she refused the cook because it would have meant leaving the wagon behind. Do you believe this?

Scene 11 is an important one. Notice how the anguish of the peasants at the thought of what will happen to their relatives in the town changes to fear that they, themselves, will be hurt. What motivates most individuals, Brecht is declaring, is their own personal safety. In a crisis, individuals do not care about the survival of society, or even of their own families. They care only about their own personal safety. We are not surprised at Kattrin's selflessness – remember how she risked her life to save the baby in Scene 5 – but we are clearly not to see her as a typical representative of humanity. For Brecht, the peasants' determination to save themselves at all costs is more typically human. Again, Brecht's view is a disturbing one, but judge whether you feel it is accurate.

The play ends on a note of pathos and harsh realism. Kattrin is killed while alerting the town, but Mother Courage will not accept her daughter's death, and sings a lullaby to her as though she were asleep. The scene is a heartbreaking one, but notice how Brecht attempts to destroy our feelings of sympathy. The peasants point out that if Mother Courage had not been away, trying to buy cheap goods, her daughter might have been saved. Examine, too, the words of the lullaby Mother Courage sings to Kattrin. She comforts herself with the thought that, while other people's children may have suffered throughout their lives, her daughter never had to. It is a selfish attitude, and Brecht intends that it should remove any feelings of pity we might have for his central character. This is why, too, Mother Courage's last words in the play are not ones of grief but a positive cry to the soldiers to wait for her, as she will soon be back in business.

Consider whether Brecht succeeds in destroying all our feelings of sympathy. Remember that Mother Courage still does not know that Eilif is dead, there is no sign of the war ending, and she has only herself to rely on. Remember, too, that she is a survivor, she does not want to die, she wants to live. Mother Courage may not be a 'heroine' in the accepted sense of the word, but neither is she a 'villain'. Could it be that she is too recognizably human?

Assignments

1 The play is one of darkness, cynicism, and despair. Is there any sense of goodness in the drama?

Suggestions for your answer:
Do you agree with the statement? Look for examples of darkness and cynicism in the play. You might refer to the war that seems to stretch on into infinity; the deaths of Mother Courage's children – and the circumstances that surrounded their deaths – and the apparent lack of any recognizable moral code. Look at the soldiers' conversations, the cook's, the chaplain's, Yvette's. What do they tell us about their situation? How do they view their lives? Is Mother Courage a cynical character, a realist, or both? There is certainly despair in the play. Is it always obviously stated, or is it sometimes hidden under a veil of black comedy? Give some examples of clear despair, and some of 'hidden' despair. Consider, too, whether you feel that Brecht, himself, despairs of mankind. Does he deliberately choose the worst traits of humanity, or is he faithfully – and despairingly – painting what he believes mankind is like?

Examine Kattrin. She is compassionate, caring, and deliberately kills herself to save others. Is she the only 'good' character in the drama? Why should she die, while others live? What lesson do you think we are to learn from Kattrin's death? That goodness cannot survive in our society, that goodness is foolhardy? Or are we to see that, despite our failings, there is humanity in some of us. Is the end of the play pessimistic or optimistic?

2 How much do you think the characters of the cook and the chaplain add to the impact of the play?

3 Imagine you are a war correspondent and have been sent to the battlefield to give your impressions. Write an imaginary interview, in newspaper form, with Mother Courage. You could ask her about her life before the war, why she is so close to danger. Perhaps you could make it a 'human interest story', painting her as a tragic figure, or would you be inclined to portray her as a calculating opportunist?

You may be studying another of Brecht's plays, perhaps *The Caucasian Chalk Circle*. Read the comments on *Mother Courage* above, and adopt similar investigative techniques for the play you are reading.

Assignments on The Caucasian Chalk Circle

1 **Is there one particular scene which you feel best illustrates the play's themes? Give a brief outline of what happens in the scene and then show how successfully, or otherwise, you feel Brecht achieves his aims.**

Suggestions for your answer:
Look for a scene in which Grusha's unselfish love and dedication, and Brecht's examination of the nature of justice, both appear. Consider how Brecht convinces us of Grusha's unswerving loyalty and devotion to Michael. What pressures are placed on her to relinquish her claim on him? Which pressure do you feel would be the hardest to withstand?

Examine the behaviour of the lawyers. Their greed is clear, their hypocrisy obvious. Azdak appears little better. Consider Brecht's ironical interpretation of the law. Who, in *law*, is rightfully the mother of the child? Legally, Azdak is wrong to give the child to Grusha, but morally he is correct. Did you expect him to behave as he did? Why, do you think, does Brecht have Azdak give this judgement? What is he suggesting to us, both about the legal system and also about his amoral character of Azdak?

2 Azdak is cynical, corrupt, and amoral. He has no 'better nature'. Do you agree?

3 The characters of Natella Abashvili and Simon contribute very little to the play. If I were producing this play I'd cut these characters out. Would you?

4 Imagine that you are Grusha. It is the end of the play. Where are you going to go now? Do you have any regrets about your way of life up to now, any fond memories of the past? Write a short story describing your thoughts and plans for the future.

Jean Anouilh

Jean Anouilh was born in Bordeaux in 1910. He studied law for a short time in Paris before entering the theatre, initially on the business rather than the creative side. Soon, however, he began to write plays and rapidly rose to prominence. Anouilh died in 1987.

His most noted works are *Antigone* (1944), *Ring Round the Moon* (1950), *Point of Departure* (1950), and *Becket* (1959).

Jean Anouilh's plays belong to the existentialist school of drama (see p. 9). His view of society and its individuals is a deeply pessimistic one. Continually in his drama there are conflicts between the beliefs of the individual and the desires of the State, and almost always the individual is sacrificed.

Moral values, too, as most people would recognize and understand them, have no relevance for Anouilh's characters. The only quality that must be preserved at all costs is one's own nature irrespective of what that nature is like. That quality – whether it is 'good' or 'bad' – is each individual's essential self.

One of Anouilh's great skills is his ability to marry cleverly reasoned argument to the framework of his plays' plots so that neither element dominates or swamps the other. Coupled to this are his strongly defined characters, with whom the reader can identify and sympathize.

Antigone

The play clearly follows the Greek dramatist Sophocles' version of the legend of Antigone, the daughter of King Oedipus of Thebes. We are told in retrospect that after the death of Oedipus, Thebes was to be ruled in alternate years by Oedipus' two sons Eteocles and Polynices. When Eteocles had reigned for a year, however, he refused to give up the throne and civil war broke out. Ultimately the two brothers fought and killed one another leaving the country to be governed by their uncle, Creon.

Anouilh's *Antigone* depicts that part of the legend when Creon has forbidden the burial of Polynices' corpse. Antigone, Polynices' sister, disobeys the order and is walled up alive in a cave where she hangs herself. Her betrothed, Haemon, the son of King Creon, overcome with grief at her death, stabs himself to death and Eurydice, Haemon's mother, cuts her own throat.

When *Antigone* was first produced in German-occupied France in 1944 it was seen by many of the French public as a defiant gesture on the part of the dramatist against the Nazi oppressors. The French saw in Antigone's stoical refusal to compromise her beliefs an expression of their own resistance to the occupation. King Creon, in contrast, represented the despised Vichy government which governed France from 1940 to 1944. The Vichy government – led by Marshal Pétain – was seen as collaborating with the Germans, prepared to make any concessions to remain in power. Ironically, the plausible, reasoned arguments Creon voices in the play were the very arguments that persuaded the Germans to allow the play to be produced at all. The Germans saw the character of Creon as Anouilh's attempt to convince his countrymen of the necessity and justification of collaboration.

Act 1

Notice Anouilh's use of a chorus. In Greek tragedy the chorus provided a moral or religious commentary on the play. In Elizabethan drama the chorus had become one person who spoke the prologue and the epilogue. The chorus as a convention fell out of favour, but was revived by several twentieth century dramatists including Eliot, Brecht, and Anouilh.

In *Antigone* the chorus is a single person who, whilst providing a commentary on the play, makes no judgement. Instead, the chorus suggests an overwhelming fatalism, almost a sense of predestination. Consider the chorus' opinions on the difference between tragedy and melodrama. In a melodrama death is appalling because there is an underlying feeling that it could have been averted, the death was premature. In a tragedy, however, the death is a peaceful conclusion to a life of trial and heartache, and therefore to be welcomed. From the chorus' words we know immediately that Antigone must die, but not how she will meet her fate.

The central core of the play takes the form of an extended debate between Creon and Antigone, as he tries to save her from death and she rejects his offer of help. The other characters in the play do not really possess independent existence, but represent the different arguments that Antigone's loved ones and the State use to try to make her change her mind.

Ismene, Antigone's sister, represents the argument of fear. She is terrified of the torture they might have to endure before they are killed, and she fears the solitude of death itself. Consider the horrifying picture she conjures up for Antigone of what their deaths could be like. The people are transformed in her mind into a great, unwashed, terrifying mob. The guards, who are Ismene and Antigone's natural protectors, develop 'idiot faces all bloated'.

From the argument of fear, Ismene then turns to that of doubt. She reminds Antigone that they did not even like their brother. What does it matter, she declares, if their brother's soul cannot rest for all eternity simply because his body is not buried? Life is too precious to be sacrificed for a brother who meant nothing to them.

Antigone can understand her sister's fears and doubts. She does not *want* to die. Notice how her fear is revealed through her conversations with her old nurse. It was the nurse who protected Antigone from harm when she was a child, but we know she cannot protect her now.

Haemon's clear love for Antigone is one of the strongest tests of her resolve. He offers her personal fulfilment, security, a family, but still she does not waver. She stretches her resolve to the limit by visiting Haemon before she buries Polynices, to request that he make love to her so that she might experience one night of love before her death, but she and Haemon quarrel.

The conversations between Creon and Antigone must be very carefully examined. Taken at surface value, Antigone can appear self-indulgent, and Creon logical and reasonable.

Creon declares that Antigone is proud and desires a spectacular death merely to satisfy that pride. Remember that Antigone went in daylight to bury her brother for the second time, almost as though she wished to be arrested. Consider how proud she appeared to be of her broken nails and bleeding fingers. Look, too, at Antigone's words to her sister Ismene, when the latter comes to tell her that she will, after all, help her to bury Polynices. Antigone is disparaging, even cruel to Ismene. Ismene, she declares, is 'blubbering'. 'You had your chance,' Antigone tells her sister twice.

In comparison to Antigone's pride, Creon appears to be a simple man. He asserts that he had no overwhelming desire to be King, and sees his position of authority in the country as similar to any tradesman with a job to do. Why do we believe him?

Notice that Creon uses Antigone's religious beliefs as a weapon and argument against her. He reminds her of the funerals they have both attended, funerals that were hurried, mumbled, meaningless. How, he declares with some justification, could such a travesty of a service be of any value for a truly loved relative? Antigone, of course, can say nothing – she knows that what he says is the truth.

Creon then asserts that as he is King – though it is an office he neither desired nor sought – he must be seen to be strong, or anarchy would ensue. Look at the metaphor of a sailing ship he employs to represent the country of Thebes. As captain of the ship, he would willingly shoot one man who disobeyed orders if that man was endangering the survival of the majority. It would not be an action he would welcome, but it would be one he would carry out if he had to. Does he appear to have a valid point?

Antigone declares that Creon could have refused the position of King, but he replies that such an action would have been cowardly. All positions of authority carry with them unpleasant duties as well as welcome advantages, and if everyone refused to take such responsibilities, society would be chaotic. To say yes, Creon declares, to take responsibility no matter what it entails, can be arduous. To say no, to give up all responsibility, is to take the easy way out.

Consider how plausible Creon's arguments are, how dreadfully rational and convincing. In comparison to them, Antigone can appear to be as Creon sees her – a wilful, stubborn, and arrogant young girl. It is only when Antigone points out that what Creon wants is a society composed of mindless, unquestioning people who, like animals, do not reason, do not think, that we realize how dangerous Creon's apparent reasonableness is.

Creon's last weapon against Antigone is his destruction of her belief in her brother. Notice how potent such a weapon is. For the first time in the play, Antigone wavers. Why should this be so? Remember she has already acknowledged that she did not like Polynices.

Examine Creon's view of life. As a youth he had been full of nobility of thought and dreams of self-sacrifice, for a just cause.

Now, he realizes that life means nothing more than the pleasure it is possible to get out of it. In the face of such cynicism, Antigone declares that if to live, to possess Creon's kind of happiness, she must compromise her ideals, must never question or defy authority, then she does not want to live. Notice that she is no longer even sure what she is dying for. She only knows that to preserve her 'self', her integrity, she cannot live.

Consider Creon's reaction to Antigone, Haemon, and Eurydice's deaths. He can see the attractions of death, of the shedding of worldly responsibilities, but he can also still justify his actions. Someone has to rule, someone has to do all the unpleasant things that no one else wants to do, just to maintain order in the land. He will compromise and compromise in order to maintain that controlled order, without realizing that he is losing himself, his own identity, in the process.

Assignments

1 Do you consider that *Antigone* is a tragedy?

Suggestions for your answer:
Look at the fate that befalls Antigone and Haemon, the two young lovers in the play. They had the possibility of a life together, but that possibility cannot become a reality. Does the fact that Antigone willingly dies lessen or increase the sense of tragedy? Remember that Antigone also represents freedom of speech and action in the play. That freedom dies with her. Do you consider that to be tragic? Creon seems so much more likeable than Antigone for most of the play. Why should that be? If Antigone was a figure of supreme nobility, with no faults, and Creon a clear villain, how would that detract from both the play's impact and the sense of tragedy? Remember that Anouilh is attacking hidden evil, evil that is more corrupting because it is not clear cut. Examine King Creon. He denies himself for expedience's sake. Is what he gains worth what he has to surrender? He would not view himself as a tragic figure. Do you? Haemon and Eurydice also die at the end of the play. Why do we not care as much about their fates as we do about Antigone's?

2 Compare and contrast Ismene and Antigone.

3 Imagine that you are Ismene. Write a short account of your feelings after the death of your sister. Perhaps you feel guilty that you are still alive, and/or angry with your sister for what she did. Remember, too, that you still live in the palace and will probably have to meet Creon daily. How are you going to cope with this situation?

Christopher Fry

Christopher Harris Fry was born in 1907 in Bristol. He worked as a schoolmaster, an actor, and a theatre director before establishing his reputation as a playwright with such dramas as *A Phoenix Too Frequent* (1946), *Thor, With Angels* (1948), *The Lady's Not For Burning* (1949), and *A Sleep of Prisoners* (1951). Fry's later plays were less successful, largely due to the fact that the popularity of poetic drama which he had been so instrumental in reviving had been superseded by the prose drama of the 'angry young men'.

Fry's most notable drama was written in a poetic form that had largely fallen out of favour in the theatre after the middle of the eighteenth century. Twentieth century playwrights who had previously attempted to reintroduce the genre had created modified speech forms of their own, as Eliot did in *Murder in the Cathedral* (1935), in case the public would not accept what had come to be considered an archaic style. Fry, however, made no such concessions. His poetic drama would have been recognizable to Jacobean audiences, and much of his success was undoubtedly due to his great skill as a poet.

Fry uses a wide range of poetic figures of speech in his drama to create extremely colourful images. His witty, epigrammatic dialogue is reminiscent of Oscar Wilde (1854–1900) and much of his drama displays a wryly cynical attitude to society.

Thor, With Angels and *A Sleep of Prisoners* have mystical and religious overtones, while *A Phoenix Too Frequent* and *The Lady's Not For Burning* are optimistic comedies with serious undertones.

Fry's characters generally believe that their lives are meaningless. They have come to this conclusion either because of temperament – they feel and care too deeply – or because society has rejected them. Love is the power which creates a glimmer of light in their darkness, love is the force which persuades them that there is some point to their existence.

The Lady's Not For Burning

The play is set in the small town of Cool Clary at the beginning of the fifteenth century, and the action covers a period of less than twenty-four hours.

Mayor Tyson's household is turned upside down by the arrival of Thomas Mendip, a one-time soldier who has come to the mayor wanting to be hanged. Mayor Tyson does not take Thomas' confessions of murder seriously, but when Jennet Jourdemayne, a local girl, is accused of witchcraft he believes that accusation without question.

Alizon Eliot is engaged to be married to Humphrey Devize, Mayor Tyson's nephew. Humphrey, however, has a brother Nicholas who, because he continually desires the same things as his brother, inevitably wishes to marry Alizon too. To further complicate matters Richard, an orphan who is Mayor Tyson's clerk, is also in love with Alizon.

Everything is eventually happily resolved. Alizon will marry Richard, Thomas decides to live after all and escapes with Jennet, and Mayor Tyson and the town of Cool Clary are left to continue as before.

Act 1

On one level the play is a romantic comedy. We suspect by the end of Act 1 that Alizon will eventually marry Richard as opposed to one of the decidedly shallow Devize brothers. We guess, too, that Thomas will rescue Jennet from burning and in the process rescue himself because – loving her – he will no longer want to die. The possible conclusion of the play, therefore, is really only of secondary interest. What gives the drama its impact is not its romantic plot but Fry's use of comedy and clever turn of phrase to contemplate serious issues.

Notice how Fry reveals the shallowness of some of the characters' religious convictions. Alizon Eliot was only given by her father to a convent because, being his sixth daughter, he was convinced he would never be able to find a husband for her. The Chaplain is vague and ineffectual, preferring the company of his viol (medieval violin) to any person. His theological knowledge is never asked for, and, on the only occasion when he tries to contradict Thomas' claim that the Day of Judgement is upon them, no one pays him any attention.

Margaret Devize appears, initially, simply a figure of fun, as she placidly and indulgently attempts to keep the peace between her two perpetually fighting sons. Consider how we learn that behind her amusing exterior lies real evil. Thomas tells her that the noise they can hear outside is a witch-hunt in progress. She replies, 'Oh! – dear; another?' Thomas is horrified by her complacency, seeing Margaret as representing the indifferent majority of mankind, interested only in what affects her personally. Her vague uninterest is as clear an indication of the evil within her as if she had been one of the mob actually hunting the witch.

Like his sister, Margaret Devize, Hebble Tyson also appears to be a humorous character in his rigid adherence to legal procedure. Thomas, he declares, cannot be hanged until he has filled in all the proper forms. The gallows is not a charitable organization that anyone can demand whenever they feel so inclined. On closer examination we see that Tyson is ruled by greed, petty mindedness and fear. Alizon's dress is only commented on because it is plainly expensive. Tyson ignores the poverty-stricken Thomas' protestations of guilt, saying he is deranged, and yet when Jennet, a girl of property, is accused of witchcraft, Tyson is all too ready to believe the accusation.

Thomas Mendip, Fry's cynical and world-weary hero, represents sensibility. He feels and cares too much for humanity. He wants to be hanged because he is tired of being constantly disappointed by mankind. He knows Jennet will be convicted, warning her ironically that innocence has never been believed by society. Tyson will convict her, Thomas declares, because he is a sadly accurate representative of mankind, who ignores real evil and yet is terrified of the unknown.

Notice that Jennet came to Tyson's house hoping for the protection of laughter – hoping that Tyson and his family would see how ridiculous the accusations against her are. Consider the irony that the one character who is truly practical and logical should be the one who symbolizes for the others the epitome of dreams and fantasy – a witch. Everyone feels a 'kind of enchantment' in Jennet's presence, but the enchantment they experience is not that of sorcery, but of someone choosing to be an individual in society. Her fanciful descriptions of nature, legends, and dreams, mark her as an outsider, and outsiders are dangerous.

Act 2

Notice that this play – with its serious undertones – is still a comedy. For Fry, laughter is God's greatest – and most inexplicable – gift to mankind. Why, Fry wonders, through his character of Thomas Mendip, should God give mankind the facility of glorious laughter, and yet also fill humanity with greed and evil?

Consider Tappercoom's comment that a belief in religion has also increased the belief in witchcraft. What statement is Fry making here about religion? Notice, too, how Tappercoom's beliefs can be twisted to suit his own ends. When the shooting star falls over Tyson's house, and the mob outside declare it to be an indication of witchcraft, Tappercoom, fearing he and Tyson may be accused, conveniently asserts that the shooting star has lost its way.

Look at the inversion of justice. Thomas is tortured to persuade him to withdraw his 'confessions', but, instead, he admits even more 'crimes'. There is, however, no monetary advantage to be gained in hanging Thomas, so Tappercoom and Tyson desperately try to find a way to make their unwelcome 'murderer' leave the town. Jennet, on the other hand, *is* wealthy, and though Tyson finds himself becoming attracted to her, he is more attracted to her money. The Chaplain comments that nothing in life is ever altogether what it appears to be. It is a sentiment that Thomas echoes when he mocks Jennet for believing in the safety of reality. Reality, we see, is whatever society chooses it to be.

Notice how Fry reveals, through the characters of Jennet and Thomas, that caring too much and caring too little are equally dangerous to the individual. Thomas wouldn't form a relationship with anyone, because he didn't want to risk being hurt. He feels too much, he cares too deeply. Jennet, conversely, shut all love out of her life, wanting only what could be scientifically proved. Both attitudes, Fry declares, are potentially destructive.

Act 3

Tyson sees danger in Jennet and Thomas. Neither conforms to what society expects, and society is much more comfortable with conformity, even if that means the humdrum, the ordinary. Notice, however, how strong the attractions of the 'different' are. Even the Chaplain is drawn to the couple, trying to play a dance tune for them so that he might see them dance together.

Richard and Alizon are the first couple to discover they love one another. Look at how that love is described. It is a love that will be a 'deep and safe place', where neither of them will ever be 'lonely any more'. Love, Fry declares, is a haven, a reason for existence in a hostile world.

Humphrey's attempt to persuade Jennet to sleep with him finally forces Jennet and Thomas to realize that they love one another. Her logic would decree that life is preferable to burning, that the loss of her virginity was a small price to pay, but she no longer thinks logically. She loves Thomas. Seeing her desperate situation, Thomas at last experiences 'the guile ... [that] ... recommends the world' – the emotion of love that can make his world endurable.

Assignments

1 Which of the character(s) did you feel most sympathy with and why?

Suggestions for your answer:
Perhaps you feel sorry for Alizon. She is either fought over or ignored for most of the play. Look at her conversations with the other characters. Do her words suggest naïvety, or wisdom, or both? Look at Richard. He is not valued by society because of his lowly birth. Examine how the other characters react to him and what he says. You may feel most sympathy for Thomas. He wants to die because he cannot bear life. Can you understand his despair at what society represents, his feeling that he cannot change the world, so he wants no part of it? Consider, however, why he does not simply commit suicide but wishes, rather, to be publicly hanged. What about the character of Jennet? She deliberately shut herself off from society, determined to live a life governed by logic. Was she really living at all? Look at the choice she is given by Humphrey. Can you understand her indecision? Was it possible to feel any kind of sympathy for the other characters in the play – are we supposed to? Remember to consider whether you *always* felt sympathy for the particular character, or whether your opinion changed as the play progressed.

2 Look at the characters of Tappercoom and Tyson. How much are they figures of fun, and how much do they represent important issues?

3 Did you find Thomas an irritating or a likeable character?

4 Write an account of the happenings at Cool Clary, as though you were Margaret Devize filling in your diary the next day. Remember the characteristics of her nature – her complacency, her involvement solely with what affects her. Remember all the people she had invited to Alizon and Humphrey's engagement party. How will she feel now that there is to be no wedding; who will she blame?

Arthur Miller

Arthur Miller was born in the Harlem district of New York City in 1915, of middle-class Jewish parents. His father was a clothing manufacturer, his mother a former teacher. After working in his father's factory Miller tried a variety of occupations before enrolling at Michigan University to study English and journalism. It was there that he began to write for the stage.

Miller's most noted plays are *All My Sons* (1947), *Death of a Salesman* (1949), *The Crucible* (1953), *A View from the Bridge* (1955) and *After the Fall* (1964).

The greatest influence upon Miller's drama was the work of the Norwegian playwright Ibsen. Like Ibsen Miller depicts his society as hostile to the individual, constricting and repressing his or her self-expression and happiness. In *Death of a Salesman* society is condemned for insisting on an image of 'success' in which money and power are the only acceptable symbols of that 'success'. In *The Crucible* Salem's inhabitants created a secure society based on religious principles in order to keep the community safe. It is that very security, however – a security which necessarily also means isolation – that allows petty jealousies and envy to grow. When the cry of witchcraft is heard, the society is all too ready to believe it and to use the opportunity to settle old scores.

As in Ibsen's drama, too, Miller's individuals are not without blame. Though the societies they live in are repressive they themselves are capable of self-delusion, cruel manipulation, and deceit. Willy Loman's life in *Death of a Salesman* is based on the illusion that he is popular and successful, and he would rather kill himself than admit this is not true. In *All My Sons* Chris' admiration for his father cannot survive his discovery that his father engaged in corrupt business dealings. In *A View from the Bridge* Eddie's obsession with Catherine leads not only to his own death but to the death of Marco and the devastation of his home.

The Crucible

For the play's setting Miller returns to seventeenth century America, to the small town of Salem in Massachusetts.

Reverend Parris' daughter Betty is ill and has been so since Parris discovered Betty, his niece Abigail, and their friends Ruth, Mary, and Mercy dancing in the forest. To save themselves from punishment – dancing is considered a sin by the community – the girls, led by Abigail, declare they are possessed by devils and accuse members of the community of bewitching them. Reverend Hale, a minister who purports to be able to detect Satanism, is sent for and trials begin in Salem.

Abigail was discharged from John and Elizabeth Proctor's service after Abigail had slept with John. To protect her husband's good name in the town, however, Elizabeth concealed the real reason why she dismissed Abigail – an action that has disastrous consequences not only for the Proctors but also for the townsfolk.

Abigail accuses Elizabeth of witchcraft, and to save his wife John at last reveals his affair with Abigail to the community, but it is too late. He is denounced by Abigail as being in league with the Devil, and subsequently hanged.

On *The Crucible*'s first production it was considered by many to have a frightening parallel to the contemporary McCarthy hearings.

Joseph McCarthy was an American judge and politician who, from 1950 to 1957, conducted what became known as a witch-hunt against supposed communists in America. By a campaign based on 'guilt by association', many famous people in Hollywood, other media personalities, and several civil servants were accused of having communist sympathies. It was an ugly time in American history. Many people were ruined, even though the charges against them were never proved. They were considered guilty simply because they had been called to appear before the House Un-American Activities Committee. Miller himself was 'investigated' and, given the date of *The Crucible* (1952), it is clear what he was attacking.

Though the direct parallel to this time in American history is no longer relevant, the play remains a powerful indictment of the nature of truth, and the corrupt misuse of power.

Act 1

It is noticeable, almost immediately, that one of the main themes of this play is 'truth'. Reverend Parris saw the girls dancing, saw his servant Tituba apparently casting spells, and saw someone running naked from the scene. He even half-suspects the real reason why Abigail was discharged from the Proctors' service. Yet this is the last time Parris will realize the truth, and, ironically, he voices that truth only to Abigail – the instigator of the lies which bring catastrophe to Salem. Consider what his reluctance to admit the truth to his congregation reveals to us, not only about him, but also about the people of Salem.

Notice the manner in which Mrs Putnam speaks of her daughter's illness. We would expect her to be worried, perhaps fearful, as she has lost so many children, but her words suggest almost a morbid pleasure in her daughter's strange behaviour. Note, too, that it was actually Mrs Putnam who sent her daughter to see Tituba, to ask her to conjure up her dead children. Mr Putnam, conversely, hardly refers to his ill daughter at all, preferring to openly delight in his minister's consternation.

Examine the conversations of Mercy, Abigail, and Betty, when they are with each other. They do not intend, initially, to be the cause of witch-hunts in Salem. What they fear is their parents' and the Church's punishment. Consider what this tells us of the community.

Notice how, on the arrival at the house of Giles Corey, Mr and Mrs Putnam, and John Proctor, the supposed fear of witchcraft in the community is replaced by petty bickering and the voicing of personal grudges and envy. Remember that all these conversations are taking place in the bedroom of an apparently very ill, 'possessed' child. Why do you feel Rebecca Nurse, the only voice of sanity in the proceedings, is ignored? Look at what is said to her, and the *way* it is said.

Examine the character of Reverend Hale. He clearly takes pride in his supposed ability to detect witchcraft. He is not a hypocrite, truly believing in the presence of the Devil amongst them, but remember that in the Christian faith pride is considered a sin. Note, too, that it is the pressure that he and Parris exert upon Abigail, to explain what she was doing in the forest, that induces her to accuse Tituba of witchcraft.

When Tituba names Goody Good and Goody Osburn as witches, remember that they are not names merely picked at random. Mr Putnam actually suggests them to her. Her so-called 'confession', therefore, arises from her desire to give those present what they want to hear.

Act 2

Look at John and Elizabeth Proctor's conversations. Notice how Miller creates the undercurrent of unspoken accusations between them. Both talk, but not about what is really important, not about what is destroying their marriage.

Mary Warren was initially determined that she would not accuse the elderly, poverty-stricken Goody Osburn. Mary attributes her change of mind to an inner conviction that Osburn *is* a witch, but examine Miller's description of the feelings she experienced during the trial. What actually motivated Mary to change her mind?

Consider the inversion of truth that is occurring in Salem. Those who confess to witchcraft are to be imprisoned, those who protest their innocence are being hanged. The law is tempting people to lie, in order to save their lives.

Notice that when the highly respected Rebecca Nurse and Martha Corey are arrested, Reverend Hale comments that 'the Devil is alive in Salem'. His words are important ones. Abigail *was* taking part in Satanic rites, so the minister's words are true, though it is completely innocent women who are on trial, not Abigail. To a non-Christian, Hale's words would simply mean that what is happening in Salem is the surfacing of the most destructive elements of mankind's nature – greed, envy, hatred and lust. To the Christian, however, the vices the townspeople display are indeed an external sign of the Devil at work, an external proof that the 'Devil is alive in Salem'. Clearly, there are different 'truths'.

Notice that when Elizabeth Proctor is arrested on the charge of making an effigy of Abigail and sticking a pin in it with intent to harm her, Reverend Hale – previously considered to be the expert on witchcraft – has to ask for the significance of the doll and the pin to be explained to him. Salem's inhabitants have all become 'experts'. Now we know why the play is called *The Crucible*. Salem has become a melting pot of emotions.

Act 3

Look at Reverend Parris' attempts to discredit Giles Corey, John Proctor, and Mary Warren. Remembering that Parris is supposedly a man of God, decide why you think he behaves in this way.

Consider what we learn of John Proctor's character from his refusal to abandon his friends. Elizabeth is safe, he does not need to stand out against authority, but he does. Notice how Deputy Governor Danforth's attitude hardens when John refuses to withdraw his accusation that the trials are based on lies. Danforth sees John's decision, not in terms of loyalty to his friends, but as a deliberate and calculated challenge to the State's authority.

Notice the irony when, for once in her life, the scrupulously honest Elizabeth lies to help her husband. Elizabeth is in prison because of Abigail's lie. If Elizabeth had told the truth about John's and Abigail's affair she would have been released, and there would have been no more witch trials. She lies to protect her husband's good name, thereby unconsciously damning, not only him, but all the others awaiting trial.

Act 4

Notice the change in Reverend Hale. His pride originally made him Salem's judge, but now, that pride is replaced by humility, as he tends to those destined to hang.

Reverend Parris reveals that Abigail and Mercy have run away, taking all his life savings with them. Why, despite this act of theft, does no one question the two girls' words regarding the people they accused of witchcraft? Remember that people have already been hanged on the strength of their testimony. Examine the inversion of truth and justice, when the Church and State attempt to persuade John to change his plea to guilty. Even Reverend Hale urges Elizabeth to try to alter her husband's declaration, commenting, with unconscious irony, that there is no principle glorious enough to die for.

Look at what actually persuades John to change his mind. It is not fear of death, or the Church, or the State, but his wife's clear love and forgiveness. Ironically, when he confesses to having seen the Devil, for John the confession is true. He always regarded Abigail as a devil tempting him, and, as he succumbed to her, he felt he *had* succumbed to the Devil. Examine why he refuses to sign a confession and ultimately goes to his death. Why should it be so important for the authorities to have a signed declaration, and yet equally important, to John, that they do not have that?

Assignments

1 Examine the play's depiction of the corrupt misuse of power.

Suggestions for your answer:
You could consider how the Church, in the forms of Reverend Hale and Reverend Parris, uses its power to influence the course of events. Do they use it in the same way, or differently? Notice that Revd. Hale initially believes there is witchcraft in Salem. Is Revd. Parris honest in his beliefs? Is Revd. Hale as guilty, in his way, for what occurs? Examine how Danforth, the representative of the State, uses his power. Is he interested in maintaining justice, do his words suggest fairness and impartiality? Is he more interested in preserving his authority than in seeking out truth? Look at the character of Elizabeth. Elizabeth has the power of giving her love and her trust to her husband, but she withholds it. How far does she – however unwittingly – create the situation, which Abigail then uses to her own advantage? Remember, too, that the girls possess a devastating power – the power of their supposed youthful innocence. Because they are young, no one suspects they may be lying. If they had been adults, would they have been so readily believed? Consider, too, the power of the community. Could people like Hale, Parris, Putnam and Danforth have possessed such power in the community, if the community had not been prepared to let them have it?

2 Is John Proctor a 'hero'?

3 Compare and contrast Elizabeth and Abigail.

4 Write your own scene in which Abigail, Mary, Mercy, Ruth and Betty make up their minds to accuse some of the inhabitants of witchcraft. Decide what their motives might be, why they choose particular people as opposed to others. Are they

malicious, evil, or does their mischief-making just get out of hand?

Many of the themes in *The Crucible* are explored, in a different way, in *Death of a Salesman*. With the aid of the investigative techniques used above, consider the following assignments.

Assignments on Death of a Salesman

1 **Examine how much of the tragedy of the play is due to the behaviour of the central character of Willy Loman, and how much of it is the result of the society he lives in.**

Suggestions for your answer:
Look at the half-truths and lies Willy tells his wife and children. He continually asserts that he is his firm's best salesman, that he is liked by everyone. He lies to himself, refusing to acknowledge that he is never going to be a success. How much happier would he have been, had he taken Charley's offer of a job and given up his illusions? Look at the effect Willy's behaviour has upon Hap. Hap uses people for his own ends and cares for no one. Would Biff have been happy with his job on the ranch if he didn't continually feel that, in his father's eyes, he was a failure? Look, too, at the society Willy lives in. What kind of values does that society have? Notice how Willy has spent all his life trying to make sufficient money to buy what his society considers 'necessities'. Willy's firm discards him, when he is worn out and exhausted, after almost thirty-six years of faithful service. How are we to judge that society? Are we to see Willy as an individual, or a representative of a particular class of society?

2 Examine the function of Linda in the play. Did you find her a likeable, admirable character?

3 Write a short essay in which Hap reveals his innermost thoughts about himself and his family. Remember that Biff appeared to be his father's favourite. Consider how Hap manipulates people at work, and in personal relationships. Is Hap content with his life?

Samuel Beckett

Samuel Barclay Beckett was born near Dublin in 1906, the second son of a quantity surveyor. After graduating from Trinity College, Dublin, Beckett taught for two terms in Belfast before going to Paris as an English lecturer. He returned to Ireland in 1930 to lecture at Trinity College, but resigned after four terms and then wandered for five years through Europe before settling permanently in France. He died in 1989.

Beckett is considered to be one of the foremost contributors to the Theatre of the Absurd (see p. 9). His most influential plays are *Waiting for Godot* (1955), *Endgame* (1958), *Krapp's Last Tape* (1958) and *Happy Days* (1961).

Beckett has a highly individual style which consists of short sentences full of constant repetition and contradiction. Comic incidents abound in his work, but as they are generally married to tragic scenes, the comedy provides not only a release but also intensifies the pathos.

Beckett's characters rarely display physical activity or have successful relationships with other people. His main concern is not with outside elements but with the development of his characters' inner selves. Any development that is made throughout a play is purely an internal one as the characters learn more about themselves.

Naturalism is rejected in Beckett's drama because he doubts whether any human being is capable of judging accurately between reality and fiction. That is why we find so many of Beckett's characters continually asking for confirmation from others that what they have seen *is* real, that what they remember happening actually *did* happen. Only by having a witness can each character confirm to themselves that *they* are real, *they* actually exist.

Time is an important element in Beckett's drama. Time passing and time refusing to pass quickly enough are continually examined, but in such a way that Beckett's characters appear to live in a world where time is meaningless. Men become blind and dumb apparently overnight in *Waiting for Godot*, and yet seem to be incapable of remembering *when* they became blind and dumb. A man talks to tapes he made of himself thirty years previously in *Krapp's Last Tape*, but these tapes are more real to him than the present. Contradictory information about past events is continually given to the audience, so that we become as disorientated about when things happened – or if they happened – as the characters on stage. This is a deliberate action on Beckett's part. For Beckett time is an illusion. Everything changes but everything stays the same.

Apart from occasional children all Beckett's characters are middle-aged or old. Youth was the time of hope and dreams, age brings with it reality, the acknowledgement of hopelessness. Beckett's view of mankind, therefore, is not of an optimistic people forging ahead towards a brighter future, but of broken-down, often physically disabled creatures lost and alone.

Waiting for Godot

Two tramps, Vladimir and Estragon, wait for someone called Godot. It appears that they have been waiting for him for a long time – it could be weeks, months, or even years. They meet Pozzo and Lucky, a master and his servant, on two different occasions. On the first occasion Pozzo is taking Lucky to the market to sell him. On the second occasion, one day later, Pozzo has become blind and Lucky is dumb. The intention to sell Lucky has either been postponed or completely abandoned. At the end of the play the two tramps promise to return again to wait for Godot.

Act 1

Notice how the very first lines of the play sum up one of the themes of the play. Estragon tries to pull off his boot. Defeated, he comments, 'Nothing to be done'. His friend Vladimir over-hears him but applies the words not to the difficulty of removing a boot but to his own life. After trying everything to make sense of, to create a purpose in his life Vladimir feels that there is nothing left to do – nothing, that is, except to wait for the mysterious Godot.

Vladimir is the practical, persistent character who, when Estragon constantly asks in despair what they are to do, replies conclusively that they must wait for Godot. Estragon is more volatile, a dreamer of dreams. Notice that one of the achievements of the play is that it manages to create dramatic action from the act of doing nothing. Vladimir and Estragon wait, and because they are waiting for someone to come they aren't technically free to go, so, in a sense, they *are* doing something.

Estragon has been beaten by a group of people who apparently continually attack him. Who these assailants are and why they habitually attack Estragon is never divulged, and we must decide for ourselves what the significance of the event is. Estragon says he was once a poet. He points ironically at his rags, asking if it isn't obvious by his poverty that he was a poet. He could be lying, of course, he could merely be the tramp he appears to be, but if he was a poet consider whether he could be beaten by members of a society who do not value artistic endeavour.

Vladimir and Estragon consider suicide as an alternative to their lives of nothingness, but we know they won't kill themselves. Not only does such a positive action seem beyond them, there is also the possibility that only one might succeed, leaving the other alone, and they fear solitude more than death.

Pozzo and the somewhat ironically named Lucky seem to be different to Vladimir and Estragon, in that they are on a journey which has a definite aim – Pozzo intends to sell Lucky at the fair. Notice that Pozzo is rich, powerful, self-assured. He reveals that in the past he learned from Lucky, and that if it hadn't been for Lucky he would never have possessed any higher thoughts. Consider the possibility that Lucky may represent Pozzo's soul. For years Pozzo has exploited and abused Lucky/his soul, and now he finds his presence irksome, because he reminds him too much of the finer person he once was.

It is possible, too, to see the relationship between Pozzo and Lucky as that of the mutual dependence of master and servant – each needs the other. Pozzo constantly asserts that Lucky is only anxious to please, so that he won't lose his position. Vladimir is horrified that Lucky is treated, and allows himself to be treated, like an animal. Consider the possibility that Beckett may be showing his contempt, both for the master race in society who exploit, and the servant class who permit themselves to be exploited.

Notice how much of the play's structure is controlled by what is an old music-hall device – the long delay. Not a single question can be answered, nor any action taken, without the maximum of argument, interruption, and confusion. It takes almost two pages of dialogue before we discover why Lucky will not put down the bags he is carrying. The shortness of most of these speeches, however, creates a sense of speed and movement in a play in which nothing concrete appears to happen.

Examine the many references made to Christ throughout this act. Vladimir recalls the two thieves who were crucified with Christ. He wonders why only one apostle mentions that one thief was given the promise of paradise by Christ. Pozzo declares that they are all made in God's image. Estragon, finding his boots are too tight for him, decides he will go barefoot as Christ did, and comments that he has always felt a special affinity with Christ.

The identity of Godot has not been revealed. Consider the possibility that he may in fact be Christ/God. Vladimir and Estragon could be waiting for God, waiting for a divinity, to give their lives on earth some meaning.

Act 2

Notice how Beckett makes us uncertain about time. The previously bare tree is now covered with leaves. Estragon can't remember whether the people who beat him today are the same as the ones who beat him yesterday. Pozzo has forgotten when he became blind and Lucky dumb, though we *think* we know they could see and speak the day before. Remember how obsessively concerned with time Pozzo was in Act 1, how often he consulted his watch, how appalled he was when he thought he'd lost it. Now blind, Pozzo has come to realize how meaningless time is. We, too, measure our lives by time, and so, by turning the play's time scale upside down, we are supposed to see how pointless such an exercise is.

Look at the way Vladimir and Estragon play 'let's pretend' games. Pretending is, in effect, what actors do, so Beckett is parodying the art of the theatre. This childish game-playing of Vladimir and Estragon, however can also be viewed as a parody of how senseless Beckett feels most adult relationships are. We conduct relationships, which can be meaningless or hurtful, simply because we cannot bear the thought of being alone.

Examine the incident when Pozzo and Lucky fall. This event can be interpreted in many ways.

Vladimir says the incident is simply a diversion in their otherwise boring lives and this is true, but look at his long speech where he condemns those who indulge in idle talk, while doing nothing for mankind. The speech is, on one level, a comic one, because *he* is doing nothing for Pozzo and Lucky. His speech, however, can also be read as a condemnation of those in positions of power who, despite seeing the need for action, remain uncommitted.

On yet another level, Vladimir and Estragon can also be seen as uncertain, would-be, Good Samaritans. In Christ's parable of the Good Samaritan, one man passed by on the other side of the road, not wanting to become involved, while the Good Samaritan went to the injured man's aid. Vladimir and Estragon neither pass by, nor help – they simply talk incessantly *about* helping. *If* Godot is in fact God, then Beckett seems to be saying that there is something fundamentally wrong with a religion which appears to be more concerned with contemplating its God than actively working for the good of humanity.

Similarly, look at Vladimir and Estragon's conversations about the dead. They conclude that living is not enough, dying is not enough. There has to be some promise of a life after death to make life worth living. Again, if we accept that Christianity is one of the underlying themes of the play, then Beckett appears to be stating that our belief in God depends solely upon His promise of immortality.

Notice how much Vladimir and Estragon need each other, and how Beckett creates almost a feeling of tenderness between the two men. They need each other as friends, they need each other as a relief from loneliness, they need each other as a witness to each other's existence, or what is apparently happening could just be a figment of their imaginations. That is why Vladimir is so often angry at Estragon's memory lapses, and why he hates him to sleep, because he needs his friend's assurances that what he thought happened, did indeed occur. Conversely, he never wants to listen to Estragon's dreams, because he cannot share them. They are unique to Estragon.

There is no feeling that Vladimir and Estragon's waiting will soon end. When night falls, and another day is over, they are either nearer to Godot's arrival, or nearer to the ultimate release of death. If we accept that Godot is God, then Beckett appears to be depicting, through the characters of his two tramps, the ultimate futility of spending a life longing for Him to take charge of our lives and destinies.

Assignments

1 A critic has said that the plot of *Waiting for Godot* consists of nothing happening, twice. Consider whether you agree with this assessment, and, if you do, whether the plot of the play is its most important aspect.

Suggestions for your answer:
Examine the actual plot of the play. Does anything happen? Time does appear to pass. Consider the changes/similarities in all four characters from Act 1 to Act 2. Pozzo and Lucky have altered physically, but have Vladimir and Estragon? Look at the four characters in detail. Were you interested in their fates? Did the fact that you know so little about their past, their motivations, affect your interest? If you consider the plot element in the play to be relatively unimportant, consider the themes Beckett incorporates into the play. The absurdity of faith, the pointlessness of life, mankind's obsession with Time, and mankind's loneliness. Examine the way Beckett portrays these themes. Look at the language he uses. Why should Beckett be so deliberately vague and uncertain, so that his play can seem to be like piecing together a jigsaw puzzle? Notice how many interpretations the play is open to. Is this a weakness, or a strength? Are Beckett's themes as important, or more important, than his characters?

2 Write a character study of Vladimir or Estragon.

3 Write a short story portraying how you imagine Vladimir and Estragon first met. Remember, that though they are tramps now, they may well have had ordinary lives at one time. What could their occupations have been? Where might they have lived? Did they have families, why did they become tramps?

4 Read another play by Beckett, and list the techniques which you feel it has in common with *Waiting for Godot*.

John Osborne

John Osborne was born in Fulham, London, in 1929, the son of a commercial artist. After a brief spell working as a journalist and then as an actor in provincial repertory companies Osborne began to write plays.

His most noted works are *Look Back in Anger* (1956), *The Entertainer* (1957), *Luther* (1961) and *Inadmissible Evidence* (1965).

Look Back in Anger is considered to be one of the most influential plays in the history of the modern British theatre. It introduced to the London stage a greater use of regional and lower-class speech habits – vernaculars which had previously been largely a feature of provincial theatres. The play also initiated the label 'angry young man', a term that was eventually applied to a particular group of dramatists of which Osborne was the leader.

Osborne and his followers were vehement in their condemnation of the chaotic mess they felt their elders had made of society. Institutions like the Law, the Church, and the Government were seen as out of touch with the lives of 'ordinary' people. Society, itself, was hostile to the individual. There was no divinity guiding or shaping mankind's fate, no hope of a happier eternity. The life that man lived now was the only one he would ever have.

With no belief in society or religion and no sense of purpose in life, the characters in Osborne's plays are lost and lonely. They search desperately for friendship and love to give meaning to their lives, but we sense that they will never find either because, emotionally, they are empty.

Physical and verbal violence are dominating elements in Osborne's work, and his skill in portraying scenes of verbal anger is his chief strength. He also displays an observant and exact ear for dialogue, an ability which enables him not only to convey anger and despair but also a darkly ironic humour.

Look Back in Anger

Alison and Jimmy are married, and live in an attic flat at the top of a large Victorian house in a Midland town. Their best friend,

Cliff, lives in the same house. Alison is pregnant, but hasn't told Jimmy. The arrival of Helena, one of Alison's friends, brings Jimmy's and Alison's marriage difficulties to a head, and Alison leaves him.

Months pass, during which time Helena moves into the flat as Jimmy's mistress, and Alison loses her baby. Alison returns to the flat, and, seeing her distress, Helena leaves, in the hope that Alison and Jimmy can salvage something from the remnants of their marriage.

Act 1

Cliff acts as a mediator, and a peacemaker, in the play. Notice that he is the one who suggests listening to the radio, going to the pub, or to the cinema – anything, in fact, to put an end to Jimmy's constant goading of Alison. Cliff also acts as Alison's confidant in the play, so that we are able to learn her innermost thoughts – a role that Helena also later fulfils. Consider, however, that though Cliff is Jimmy's closest friend, Jimmy never confides in him. All that we know of Jimmy's thoughts is either gleaned from his very public conversations or from other people's interpretations of his behaviour.

While Alison does not often react to Jimmy's verbal abuse, she *is* capable of retaliation. Notice how she scotches Jimmy's fond reminiscences of his mistress, Madeline. She is not a 'doormat', and yet when Jimmy condemns her parents as malicious, and her brother as a stupid member of the Establishment, who not only does not want change in society but cannot see the need for it, she doesn't reply. Consider the possible reasons for her silence. Perhaps Jimmy's verbal abuse happens so frequently that she no longer hears anything he says. She could also know that Jimmy is only content if he can get her to react, and she has decided not to give him the satisfaction of seeing just how upset she is. Consider, too, the possibility that, after so many years of living this way, it is simply easier for her to say nothing.

Notice how Jimmy continually provokes confrontation. For him, silence and harmony do not suggest internal peace, but sterility. He thrives on argument – even an argument over something as trivial as who will make the tea.

From his scathing attitude towards his wife's background, we assume, initially, that Jimmy is working-class, but notice that

Cliff – who *is* working-class – reveals that Jimmy's relatives on his mother's side of the family are 'posh'. Jimmy reads 'posh' Sunday newspapers, considering them the only newspapers with anything intelligent to say. He is arrogant, too, about his intelligence, declaring that only he – unlike Cliff and Alison – actually understands what he reads.

Despite his pride, arrogance, and inverted snobbery, consider how insecure he is. Though he is sarcastic about Alison's father nostalgically looking back to the Edwardian era, he actually envies him. The picture Colonel Redfern has of life before the First World War may be romanticized, but at least he has that. Jimmy has nothing. Nothing to look forward to, nothing to look back on. He is not even sure of his relationship with Alison. He searches her handbag daily, and examines all the cupboards for evidence that she is betraying him in some way.

Notice, too, that his wife's love for him is not a source of pleasure to him. Sex, for Jimmy, is not a fulfilment but a death, a loss of his own identity. Decide why he cruelly tells Alison – albeit without knowing she is pregnant – that he wishes she could have a child and that it would die. Why should he believe Alison needs to suffer the pain of loss in order for her to become a 'real' human being? Look at his own anguish. He is adrift in a society he despises but cannot change.

Act 2 Scene 1

Consider how much of a fraud Jimmy is. His background is, in its way, as privileged as Alison's. Not only are his relatives comfortably off, as we have already learned, he is also university educated. Notice, too, that though he blames Alison for his friend Hugh leaving the country without him, he actually refused to go, saying that Hugh was giving up the social struggle and abandoning his mother.

Examine Alison's revelations about the parties she, Jimmy, and Hugh used to gatecrash. The hosts of these parties knew Alison's parents, and were too polite to throw them out. Consider what Jimmy and Hugh meant to achieve by these 'victories' over a society they despised – victories that really only consisted of the amount of embarrassment they caused.

Jimmy's memories of his father's death are coloured by anger, despair, and hopelessness. Alison believes Jimmy *wants* to suffer, wants to feel pain, as a form of self-punishment. He couldn't help his dying father; he wants to be working-class, but isn't. He runs a sweet-stall, thereby deliberately denying his intellectual capabilities. It seems that he must punish himself for belonging to a privileged class, for not having a cause to fight for as his father did in Spain. How much of this do you think Jimmy, himself, is aware of?

Notice how angry, abusive, and violent Jimmy appears. He warns Helena, twice, that if she strikes him he will hit her back. Why, then, do you think he doesn't retaliate, but collapses, when Helena slaps his face?

Act 2 Scene 2

Osborne subtly turns our attention away from Jimmy, as being the main cause of the breakdown of the marriage, and directs us towards an examination of Alison. Cleverly, Osborne chooses an unlikely agent in the form of Alison's father. Colonel Redfern reveals that he blames his daughter for the collapse of the marriage. We have seen that Jimmy is not all that he appears to be, and now we are forced to recognize that Alison, too, is not honest.

Remember, in Act 2 Scene 1 Alison told Helena that she believed Jimmy married her simply because her parents were so horrified at the prospect of him as a son-in-law. Consider whether Alison's parents' opposition to the marriage also constituted one of the main reasons why *she* wanted to marry *him*. She was rebelling against her parents' values, and yet, as her father points out, she didn't maintain her act of defiance. She continued writing to her parents, she maintained the link, even though it meant being disloyal to her husband.

Act 3 Scene 1

Cliff is moving out, and wants to dissolve the sweet-stall partnership he has with Jimmy. Notice Cliff's unconsciously ironic comment when he tells Jimmy that such an occupation suits Jimmy, because he is university educated, but he wants something better.

Examine the relationship Jimmy has with Helena, and compare it to the one he had with Alison. What are the similarities/differences?

Jimmy still dreams of finding a cause worth dying for. Notice that he seldom sees himself as being instrumental in changing society – death in a glorious fight is preferable to contributing to political or social change. What does this tell us about his character?

Act 3 Scene 2

Alison claims not to want to break up Helena and Jimmy's relationship. Do you believe her? Notice that she once changed her seat in the cinema to be nearer to a man smoking Jimmy's brand of tobacco. She knows, too, that Helena is a Christian, and must be guilt-ridden, not only at living with a married man but also at living with a man whose wife has lost her baby. Alison says she has returned to the flat to see if the place where she endured so much really does exist. *Is* that why she has come back?

Alison has suffered the pain and loss Jimmy wanted her to have. There is almost a sense of her having revelled in that loss. She has endured what Jimmy wanted her to. She is equal to him now.

Look at the end of the play. Is it optimistic, or do we sense that they are two broken people, still searching for fulfilment, still looking for an answer to their lives? They may not find what they are searching for, but can they find some kind of consolation in each other?

Assignments

1 **Write about the play's treatment of love.**

Suggestions for your answer:
Examine the relationship between Jimmy and Alison. Does Jimmy love her, and does she love him? Consider their conversations, and what they say about each other to the other characters in the play. Do they appear to be a 'normal' husband and wife? Is love more important for Jimmy, or for Alison? Do you feel that they both share the same expectations of love?

Look at the relationship between Helena and Jimmy. Did you feel that either of them expected the relationship to last? Did they want the same things from the relationship? Did you admire either Jimmy or Helena for the way they behaved when their relationship was over, or did you feel that neither was truly honest about their feelings? Examine the relationship between Cliff/Alison/Jimmy. Which character – if any – did you feel cared the most selflessly about the others? How is this revealed to us by Osborne? Does Cliff's presence help Jimmy and Alison's marriage, or does it hinder it?

2 In what ways is Jimmy Porter repulsive?

3 Compare and contrast Alison and Helena. Which character do you feel is more honest?

4 Write a letter from Alison to Helena, in which she tries to explain to her friend why she will stay with Jimmy.

You may be studying John Osborne's *The Entertainer* rather than *Look Back in Anger*. Some of the themes and types of character explored in the latter are very similar to those examined in *The Entertainer*. Using the techniques employed in the assessment of *Look Back in Anger*, answer the following assignments on your play.

Assignments on The Entertainer

1 Which character(s) did you feel most sympathy with in the play and why?

Suggestions for your answer:
Firstly, remember to take note of whether you *always* felt sympathy for that character or characters, or whether your opinion changed. Consider *what* changed your opinion.

Examine the character of Jean. Look at her revelations of her relationship with her fiancé, her life away from home. Now examine her conversations with the individual members of her family. How does she view them, and how do they see her? Does she feel truly complete and fulfilled with Graham, with society, with her family? Whose fault is this – Graham's, society's, her family's, or her own?

Examine the character of Archie. He tries to hold on to the remnants of his past glory on the stage, and can't accept that he is no longer wanted. Did you feel sympathy for him? Examine his relationship with his family, and in particular with his wife and Billy. He uses people. Does that colour your opinion of him?

Has society treated Archie fairly, or do you feel that he has got no more than he deserves?

Did you find Phoebe irritating, or moving, or both? Why? How does Osborne influence your opinions of her? Look at her treatment of Jean, and then look at her behaviour to the other members of the family.

Look at Billy. What was your initial opinion of him? Did it alter in any way as the play progressed?

2 Billy and Archie were both entertainers. In what ways are they similar as people, and in what ways different?

3 Imagine that you are Phoebe. Write a letter from her to Jean, describing your new life in Canada, what Archie is doing now, whether you have any regrets about leaving Britain. Remember the kind of character she is in the play, and try to reproduce her uncertainties, her slowness, her repetitiveness, in your letter.

4 Compare and contrast either of these plays with another play by John Osborne, or with a play by another dramatist writing in the same period, i.e. late 1950s – 1970s.

Harold Pinter

Harold Pinter was born in the East End of London in 1930.

His most noted works to date are *The Room* (1951), *The Birthday Party* (1958), *The Dumb Waiter* (1960), *The Caretaker* (1960), *The Collection* (1961), and *The Homecoming* (1965).

Pinter's methods of characterization are very different to those of previous dramatists. Earlier playwrights give, within the first few moments of the action, all the information – origin, background, motivations – needed for an audience to understand and categorize the characters they see. With Pinter's characters, however, there is always an element of uncertainty about their motivations and also of their backgrounds. Pinter declares that as we cannot say with any degree of certainty what our own motives always are, nor those of our closest family, why should we be supplied with – and, indeed, expect to be supplied with – a complete profile for a character we encounter for one evening on a stage?

Just as the information we have about Pinter's characters is sparse so, too, are his stage settings, which normally consist of just one room. Generally his characters are afraid of what lies beyond the room, afraid of the outside world, seeing any intrusion into their room from the outside as an invasion of their privacy and safety. (*The Homecoming* is one of Pinter's few exceptions to this generalization in that the position here is reversed. The danger exists *in* the room and the victim comes from the outside.)

Few dramatists have had a form of dialogue named after them, but the term 'Pinteresque' has come to signify a very specific form of language. Repetition, self-contradiction, recurrent tautologies (the saying of the same thing twice over in different words) are all hallmarks of Pinter's dialogue.

Allied to and an integral part of this particular dialogue is an acute ear for the colloquial coupled with a great awareness of the theatrical significance and impact of silence. Pinter realized that characters saying nothing at all at key moments could be just as significant or meaningful as if they had spoken at length.

By means of this specialized dialogue Pinter creates suspense, ambiguity, uncertainty. Is the old man in *The Caretaker* really called Davies or is he called Jenkins? Why is Stanley in *The Birthday Party* being pursued by Goldberg and McCann? Who is the 'he' Gus and Ben refer to in *The Dumb Waiter*, almost as though he were their controller? Pinter does not raise these questions with a view to answering them. What matters for him is 'now', and what is going to happen next. The past, he feels, is coloured, distorted, by different people's recollections of it – there is no single truth, no one reality of past events.

Women are not treated kindly by Pinter. Female characters in his plays are either crushingly possessive mother figures or tarts, and both types talk incessantly and never listen. Meg in *The Birthday Party* is a rather cruel portrayal of an essentially feeble-minded elderly woman. In *The Homecoming* and *The Room* Ruth and Rose are highly unsympathetic characterizations.

The Birthday Party

The Birthday Party was Pinter's first full-length play.

Stanley Webber, a man in his thirties, has a room in a seedy seaside boarding house where he is looked after with smothering intensity by the landlady, Meg, a simple elderly woman. Goldberg and McCann, the two representatives of an unidentified and brutal organization, arrive to take Stanley away. Petey, Meg's husband, and Lulu, the girl next door, complete the dramatic cast.

The action of *The Birthday Party* covers twenty-four hours, during which time we witness Stanley being given a birthday party, though it obviously isn't his birthday, and then being verbally and physically battered into silence by McCann and Goldberg before he is taken away by them to an unknown destination.

Act 1

In Act 1 we meet Meg, Petey, and Stanley having breakfast. Look at the conversations between Meg and Petey, and Meg and Stanley. On the one hand they consist of the commonplace utterances people make to each other, but they also reveal the different relationship Meg has with Petey to the one she has with Stanley. Consider, too, Pinter's repetitive use of the word 'nice'. Sometimes it is plainly meant to mean just what it says, a trite compliment, but on other occasions Pinter uses the word ironically and menacingly.

We learn that Stanley came to the seaside resort as a pianist for the concert party who played at the pier. He hasn't worked now for months, rarely goes out, and though he is contemptuous of Meg and sometimes cruel to her, he is also dependent on her. Consider the wheelbarrow incident. Does Stanley suggest it might be a coffin to frighten Meg, or is he projecting his own nightmare, or are both interpretations justified?

Stanley feels rejected by the world. He says that he once gave a very successful concert, but that when he arrived at the venue for his second concert, the hall was closed. This incident could be true or it could be a fantasy. Stanley plainly believes it. Notice how convinced he appears to be that the hall's closure was not simply due to an oversight on somebody's part. 'They'd locked it up', 'they carved me up', 'they pulled a fast one'. Consider why the vagueness of the identity of these people should seem more terrifying to him and us than if 'they' were actually identified.

Lulu is interested in Stanley but he rejects her advances despite the fact that she is single and closer to him in age than Meg is. What does this tell us about Stanley?

The two men who come to the boarding house – McCann and Goldberg – ostensibly looking for rooms, are identified by Pinter as an Irishman and a Jew respectively. Combined with the character of Stanley, we have the stock musical hall joke ingredients – 'There was an Englishman, an Irishman, and a Jew', etc. Consider why Pinter should create what appears to be a scenario for humour when the real situation turns out to be anything but.

Goldberg and McCann's conversations exhibit Pinter's ambiguous style. Their words can be as innocent as they initially appear or they can project dark undertones.

GOLDBERG: Everywhere you go these days it's like a funeral.
MCCANN: That's true.

Look for other examples of this ambiguity.

Meg's present to Stanley is a child's drum. Stanley is a musician, so the choice of gift is doubly tragic for him – the child's drum suggesting both that his professional playing days are over and underlining Meg's view of him as a child. He accepts the gift, but consider why he should begin to beat it so savagely.

Act 2

In Act 2 Stanley finally meets McCann and Goldberg. There is a suggestion that Stanley recognizes McCann when he asks him if he has ever been in Maidenhead, citing Fuller's teashop and a Boots' library as landmarks. McCann denies ever having been in Maidenhead but later in this act we hear *Goldberg* reminiscing about having tea at Fuller's and taking a library book from Boots. *Do* these men know each other, or is this just a meaningless coincidence, or is Goldberg lying? Goldberg's truthfulness is certainly not beyond question. Look at the story he tells McCann about his mother and the gefilte fish, and compare it to the story he tells Lulu about his wife and the roll-mop and pickled cucumber.

Once McCann and Goldberg have Stanley alone they fire a flood of apparently meaningless questions at him. The words in themselves are not frightening, so consider how Pinter creates a sense of menace. Notice the speed of the questions, the impossibility of anyone being able to answer some of them. Stanley becomes more and more bewildered, more and more confused under the attack because words – our source of communication – fail him. Notice, too, that there is humour in some of the questions McCann and Goldberg ask. The laughter created is plainly a safety device for the audience. Remember that the play is meant to be seen. To watch a person being systematically broken is harrowing in the extreme and some kind of release is essential.

McCann and Goldberg are not equal partners in this enterprise. Consider who is the instigator of each 'attack', which man seems more in control both of himself and the situation.

The game of blind man's buff ends Stanley's birthday party catastrophically. While blindfolded Stanley accidentally steps onto his new drum, destroys it and, in the process, symbolically destroys the last vestige of his status as a musician. Consider what else this incident could signify. Notice, too, that though it has been McCann and Goldberg who have, since their appearance, threatened physical violence, it is Stanley who actually commits the violence at the end of Act 2, attempting to strangle Meg and attacking Lulu. He is the one who has lost all restraint, he is the one who has broken.

Act 3

Compare the description we are given of Stanley in this act to the one we are given in Act 1. We would expect that a person who has had a nervous breakdown would allow his outward appearance to deteriorate, whereas an adjusted person would be well groomed. Notice how Pinter overturns our preconceptions by reversing the situation. He will not let us neatly categorize anything or anyone.

Goldberg and McCann subject the now speechless Stanley to further barrages of words. Consider how the words, this time, are not couched in questions but statements, statements which appear on the surface conciliatory, concerned with treatment, recuperation and recovery. The words, however, are still used as weapons, so why do you think Pinter changes his approach here?

Was it a surprise to you when Petey attempted to protect Stanley? Previously he was portrayed as a weak character. How much of the truth do you think he knows, or is he simply trying to help someone even weaker than himself?

Assignments

1 To what extent – if any – do you think Pinter's economical representation of character, plot and motivation, adds to, or detracts from, the play's impact?

Suggestions for your answer:
Remember that the play is an intensely dramatic one. Fear of the unknown can be much more devastating than a concrete fear. If we knew why Goldberg and McCann wanted Stanley, we would have clearer motivations, but would the tension be lessened or increased? Look at the language they use to each other, and the language they use to Stanley. What are the differences and similarities? Why should this be so? Are they friends, colleagues, or both? Consider Stanley. Do we actually *need* to know more about him, to care about what happens to him? Did you feel he was a 'real' person, or is Pinter's style so sparing that Stanley becomes a 'cardboard' figure? Stanley has friends, a past – however vague – and hopes and dreams. Is this enough?

At the end of the play, did you feel satisfied, or were you left with unanswered questions? Does it matter that the play's conclusion is not neatly tied up?

When Stanley smashes his drum, and attacks Lulu, were you

surprised by his actions? Remember that Pinter believes that no one ever truly *knows* anyone else. He is stressing the uncertainty of life itself.

2 What function do you think the character of Petey performs in the play?

3 Pinter claims that he is dealing with characters who are at essential turning points in their lives. Which of the character(s) would you say were at a turning point?

4 How do you think Meg will justify Stanley's disappearance to herself? Write the scene that you imagine might take place between Petey and Meg, or write the entry Meg might make in her diary concerning the events that have occurred.

You may be studying a different Pinter play. Look at the themes, characterizations and theatrical techniques Pinter employs in *The Birthday Party*. Look for similar and different presentations in the play you are examining, and then try to carry out the following assignments.

Assignments on The Caretaker

1 Consider the ways in which the play is humorous, tragic, and frightening.

Suggestions for your answer:
You could examine the character of Davis. His exaggerations are comic; so, too, is his self-importance. Look behind the image he projects. What is the *reality* of his situation? Has he family, friends? When he is told to leave, what kind of future does he face? Notice, too, how he deliberately tries to drive a wedge between Aston and Mick. Why does he do this? Is it purely because he is malicious?

Look at Aston. He has good intentions, he has difficulty making friends. His room is full of assorted pieces of junk, which, while appearing worthless, clearly mean something to him. Are we to see him as a humorous character, or a pathetic character, neither, or both?

Mick continually teases Davis and the situation is amusing, but notice how quickly he becomes a figure of menace. How does Pinter create this atmosphere of fear? Is what Mick actually *does* frightening, or is it the uncertainty of what he *might* do that creates the feelings of menace in the play?

2 Which character, would you say, was *least* successfully drawn by Pinter and why?

3 Imagine that you are Davis or Aston. Write a conversation with a stranger in which you give *your* account of what happened at the house. Remember to keep in character. If you choose Davis, remember how much he exaggerates, and how frequently he lies. You/he will want to appear to your/his advantage in the story. If you choose Aston, remember to mirror his vagueness about everything, his kindness.

Assignments on The Homecoming

1 Does Pinter's economical style succeed in this play, or is it, in fact, one of its weaknesses?

Suggestions for your answer:
Pinter intends to draw a parallel between Max and his wife, and Ruth, but is he successful? Max seems to have no humour. Does this make him more effective as a figure of menace, or does he become too one-sided because of it? Pinter is deliberately vague about Teddy and Ruth's presence in England. Is this vagueness effective, or does it make their visit appear too improbable? Is there a sense that some of Pinter's speeches are deliberately mystifying, included simply for their effect, as opposed to creating a specific atmosphere? Conversely, does such vagueness intensify the play's dramatic effect? Do any incidents occur that are *too* unexpected? Examine the scene between Ruth and Lenny. Was there any indication of sexual attraction between the couple before?

2 Uncle Sam is too much of a weakling. I despise him, and feel he deserves everything he gets. Do you?

3 If you were asked to produce this play, are there any incidents you would be tempted to cut? Why?

Robert Bolt

Robert Oxton Bolt was born in Manchester in 1924, the son of a shopkeeper. He worked in an insurance office and then as a schoolteacher before the success of his play *Flowering Cherry* in 1958 encouraged him to devote himself full time to writing.

His most noted plays to date are *Flowering Cherry, The Tiger and the Horse* (1960) and *A Man for All Seasons* (1960).

Though not a supporter of any one political party, Bolt is vehemently committed to the abolition of nuclear weapons and has served a short term of imprisonment because of his involvement in the cause of nuclear disarmament. Given such strength of feeling it is not surprising that his plays often have as an underlying theme the conflict between the rights of the individual and the rights of the state.

Bolt's plays are deceptively simple in construction with tight-knit plots. Despite his frequent use of the extended metaphor this device in no sense obscures Bolt's text but rather adds a richness of dimension by reinforcing the theme of the play.

A Man for All Seasons

Henry VIII wants to divorce his wife Catherine of Aragon in order to marry Anne Boleyn. Although she has a daughter Mary, Catherine has been unable to give Henry the male heir he wants and is now presumed to be barren. Henry VIII approaches the Pope to ask for the marriage to Catherine to be annulled on the grounds that, as he had married his brother's widow, he had contravened Christian law. As the Pope had originally issued the dispensation to allow Henry to marry Catherine he naturally refuses to overturn his earlier ruling. When Henry decides that the Pope is nothing more than the Bishop of Rome and therefore has no jurisdiction over him, the split from the Catholic Church is inevitable.

Against this background we have the figure of Thomas More, the Lord Chancellor, who steadfastly refuses to give his approval to Henry's marriage to Anne Boleyn, and is eventually executed.

Act 1

Notice that the historical events Bolt depicts are actual and not imaginary. The play, therefore, does not depend for its interest, or impact, upon the plot. What interests us – and indeed Bolt – are the motivations of the characters, their relationships with each other, and the society they inhabit.

The Common Man appears in a variety of roles throughout the play – a boatman, a gaoler, a steward, the prologue, etc – but he always maintains the same wryly cynical attitude to life and humanity. He represents what is common to all but a few of us – our ability to distance ourselves from possible trouble. We will be kind and tolerant, but only so long as our own lifestyle is not threatened. We will stand up for our rights, but not to the point when society might ostracize us. The Common Man recalls Brecht's alienation (see pp. 2–3) effect, since he is both in the play, and outside of it.

Richard Rich is an opportunist. He believes that everyone has their price, that there is no ideal a man may hold which he would not surrender if sufficient monetary reward were offered. He uses his friendship with More as a tool, to try to gain the social position he desires, but More has no illusions about Rich's loyalty and friendship. Consider whether More is foolish to allow such a man to be so close to him, or whether he is merely realistic, sensing that society is largely composed of such people.

Rich progresses in this act from the somewhat naïve young follower of More – consider how potentially dangerous to himself some of his comments are – to the apparently more worldly person he appears with Cromwell. Notice, however, that he has no ideals. He will do anything, be anything, in order to gain what he wants. Though he may rise, socially and materially, throughout the play, *he himself* does not grow, because he has no 'self'.

Wolsey, Roper, and More, are the representatives of the Church in the play, but you should examine the differences between the three men's beliefs.

Wolsey's views on the royal divorce are not religious, not moral, but practical. His King desires a divorce, and, for Wolsey to maintain his position in society, it is imperative that the King has what he wants. In society's terms, Wolsey is much more of a realist than More, but consider whether he is truly a churchman.

Roper, whom More's daughter Margaret wishes to marry, is committed to the form of worship most under attack at any given time. At the beginning of Act 1, he is a Lutheran, because the members of that Church are being reviled, but, when the Catholic Church becomes the target of abuse, he begins to modify his views. We sense that, by the end of the play, he will probably be the most vocal champion of Catholicism. Consider why Roper continually changes his allegiance. Is it because of considered, reasoned thought or because he is attracted by the mental picture of himself as a martyr, reviled by society, and therefore, in his eyes, superior to it?

More's religious views are simple, uncomplicated, and as much a part of him as his own features. He can see, all too clearly, the irony of defending a Church whose head is corrupt, but this in no way lessens his fundamental beliefs. His beliefs are *him*. To alter, or remove them, would destroy him.

Examine how the different factions of society interpret More's refusal to agree to what King Henry wants. Chapuys, the Spanish ambassador, sees More's decision as a political one, an indication to the world of his support for Catherine of Aragon and Spain. Wolsey sees More's refusal merely as an indication of More's overwhelming pride and arrogance. Henry VIII believes that, as he and More were friends, More should display the loyalty one would expect from a friend. Alice, More's wife, senses that their world is disintegrating, and believes that it is essential for their family's safety that her husband does not stand out alone against society. What do these different interpretations of More's actions tell us about More's society?

Consider how More places his faith in the law coming to his aid, forgetting that the law is a product of, an instrument of, the State. When his family urge him to have Rich arrested because he is a danger to them, More replies that, as Rich has broken no law, he can do nothing. If he bends the law, he declares, he can hardly protest if others do likewise. What do we learn of More's character, and the values of society, from this incident?

Notice how much Bolt's use of imagery adds to the impact of Act 1. Water – the sea, rivers, currents – is used continually as a metaphor for religion, faith. Rich has none, he is 'adrift'. More is always seasick, so we know that he will be unable to keep up with the changing tide/religious opinion. The River Thames becomes deeper and more dangerous every day, just as the complex questions of Church and Monarch become increasingly complicated. The land, conversely, symbolizes society, and this is where More feels safe. He does not want to stand alone, outside of society, and believes he can hide within 'the thickets of the law'.

A close examination of the dialogue also reveals underlying meanings. Cromwell's question to Rich, 'Are you coming in my direction?', can mean just what it seems to, but it can also imply a political question – are you *my* man, can I rely on your help? When the Steward sees More giving Rich a cup simply because he asks for it, he notes sagely that his master has a dangerous habit. At some point, More might be asked to give something he wants to keep. The comment can mean that More might have to give up something of great monetary value, or, that he might be required to relinquish his integrity, his self.

Act 2

The political, religious, and family pressures upon More have intensified. Society has now distanced itself from More. Notice that he can't even get a boatman to take him down river, because it is dangerous to be seen in his company. His actions are seen by the Catholic Church as an indication to the world that the Roman Catholic Church is the only true church. His own family resent their straitened circumstances, and cannot understand why he cannot simply agree to what the English Catholic Church and King want.

Notice that More does not stand out alone against society because of any saintly qualities. He has difficulty in removing his chain of office, because he is human enough to have greatly enjoyed the social advantages it brought. He displays jealousy, when he tells Norfolk he must watch the north of the country in case of possible insurrection, and then discovers that Norfolk already knows this. We are not to see More as a man without faults, a man superior in every way to his society. What makes him unique in his society is his unswerving determination to maintain his integrity, no matter what the cost to himself.

When More is imprisoned, which member of his family comes closest to altering his resolve? Examine Margaret's and Alice's conversations with More. He plainly adores his clever daughter, and their conversations in Act 1 appeared to satisfy him much more than those with his rather plain-spoken, slightly nagging wife. When he faces death, however, it is Alice's distress at his abandonment of her for what she deems a meaningless gesture, Alice's plain, honest, love for him, that almost proves his undoing.

At More's trial, his belief that the law will be his shield, his protector, is finally destroyed. Notice that, ironically, the law is actually deliberately perverted to convict him. More knows that, in law, silence is always understood to imply consent, but Cromwell declares that More's silence indicates his opposition. Richard Rich – now Sir Richard Rich, the Attorney General for Wales – lies under oath about conversations he and More had while More was in prison. Too late, More sees how fragile the protection of the law is for an individual who decides he must stand out against the might of the State.

Assignments

1 'The conflict in the play arises from the failure of More to recognize the truth, not only about himself, but also about the society he is part of.' Discuss whether you accept this assessment of the play.

Suggestions for your answer:
Consider More's character. He is a man who has risen to the position of Lord Chancellor, a post requiring not only ability but also the approval of his society. Is he naïve, or arrogant, or both, not to see that his high social rank inevitably puts him in a position where *any* decision he might make would be remarked upon? Does he realize that his values are not the values of his society? More clearly does not understand that his society, and its laws, are only as strong as the individual members who make it up.

Look at the other characters in the play. If you had been More, would you have expected Richard Rich to stand by you? Did More expect him to? What kind of character is Norfolk? Does he care about his social status as much as Rich does? Look at all of Norfolk's conversations with More. Would Norfolk have stood out, like More, from the rest of society?

Examine Cromwell and Wolsey's actions. How much does expedience play in their decisions?

Are we to see Rich, Cromwell, Wolsey, and Norfolk, as particularly evil men, or do they simply represent society as a whole?

2 Given that the play is a re-enactment of an historical event, consider whether you feel that it has any relevance for us today. Give your reasons clearly.

3 Compare and contrast the characters of Margaret and Alice.

4 Write a letter from Alice More to the Duke of Norfolk after her husband's death. Remember the different emotions that she may be experiencing – unhappiness, despair, anger, at her husband and the State. She might recall former, happier times the Mores and Norfolk shared. She would certainly be unsure about her future. She could go and live with Margaret and her husband, but would they get on each others' nerves?

Peter Shaffer

Peter Shaffer was born in 1926 in Liverpool. His most noted plays to date are *Five Finger Exercise* (1958), *The Royal Hunt of the Sun* (1964), *Black Comedy* (1965), *Equus* (1973), and *Amadeus* (1979).

Shaffer's main concern in his serious drama is the portrayal of individuals who are isolated from their societies, either because of their temperament, or because the societies they inhabit are alien to them. Continually these characters strive to find some means of identification for themselves that is not dependent upon conforming to what their society wishes them to be. They are individualists in societies that demand conformity.

Shaffer's style is a tightly structured one. His stage directions are complex and detailed, his plots rounded and deceptively simple.

The Royal Hunt of the Sun

The play depicts the Spanish conquest of Peru – specifically the land ruled by Atahuallpa – by Francisco Pizarro and his men. The Spanish soldiers go on the expedition seeking gold, the Church accompanies Pizarro to bring the 'heathen' to Christ, and Pizarro hopes that in this new world he may find a reason for his existence.

Atahuallpa does not fear the Spaniards, believing they are gods like himself. As a god meeting other gods, he comes to see Pizarro unarmed and is captured after three thousand of his people are massacred. Pizarro promises to release Atahuallpa if he can fill a room full of gold, but it is a meaningless promise as Pizarro does not for one moment believe that such an achievement is possible. To Pizarro's amazement and consternation, however, Atahuallpa does indeed do the impossible. Atahuallpa cannot remain indefinitely in prison, but nor can he be released because, once freed, he would raise an army against the Spaniards. Atahuallpa must die.

Act 1

Examine the description of the stage setting at the beginning of this act — four black crucifixes which are sharpened to resemble swords. Consider what kind of statement Shaffer is making here about the Spaniards' Christianity, even before the play has begun.

Notice how this linking of the Spaniards' Christianity to pain and death is reinforced throughout Act 1. In Scene 4, Fray Valverde refers to the Indians they capture as 'pagan dust' who must be shown no 'softness'. In Scene 12, it is the priests who urge their army to kill Atahuallpa's followers, because of Atahuallpa's supposed act of 'blasphemy' when he throws the Bible from him in disgust. Clearly, one of the themes of the play is whether there can ever be any moral justification for one group of people — no matter how well intentioned — to forcibly impose their beliefs upon others.

Consider how young Martin reminds Pizarro too much of the idealistic young man he once was, a young man whose ideals Pizarro now regards as foolish and naïve. Clearly, Martin's journey to Peru will be a journey of self-discovery and knowledge, but will it be a knowledge that he will want to have?

Pizarro is a self-made man, acutely aware of his illegitimacy and his poverty-stricken background in a society where birth and wealth are all-important. He has no illusions left about mankind and, most importantly for him, no religious faith. Look at his ironic view of the priests and their beliefs in Scene 4, when he declares that their Christ is a man of 'shackles and stakes', their God a God of 'big cannon to blow [the Indians] out of the sky'.

Examine Pizarro's view of society. He believes that because the world is so vast and terrifying, man creates smaller social groups so that he feels less intimidated and alone. The social groups Pizarro identifies are the Court, the Army, and the Church. Because of his birth and temperament, Pizarro is excluded from these groups. He is isolated, rootless, and has no place in the world. Rejected by, and rejecting, society Pizarro strives for a fame that will give him immortality, so that he will no longer need society.

Consider the description Pizarro gives us of the Spanish society. It is class-ridden and wealth-orientated, but it does provide the opportunity for an individual – albeit with difficulty – to make his name. Compare this society to the description we are given in Scene 6 of the Indian culture. The society is rigidly controlled. Each month is dedicated to a specific task, each age is allotted a particular duty. There is no place for individuality, but there is also no poverty or greed. De Soto, Pizarro's second-in-command, envies this Indian society, seeing it as providing the answer to the horrors of grinding poverty, covetousness and envy, which are the hallmarks of the Spanish society.

Note the early indications in Scene 4 that we are to consider Atahuallpa in Christ-like terms. He is the Sun God's child, who is sent to earth for a few years of his life before he must return to his father's world, where he will live for all eternity.

Act 2

For young Martin, the massacre of Atahuallpa's followers also means the destruction of his own ideals. He had seen himself as 'the very perfect knight Sir Martin' – a clear echo of Chaucer's chivalric 'verray parfit gentil knight' in the *Canterbury Tales* – but he cannot find any glory in the killing of unarmed men. De Soto points out to him that, if the Spaniards had been massacred, the Indians would never have had the opportunity to hear the word of God. There is a kind of logic in De Soto's words, but consider whether the Spaniards' actions were justifiable in the light of their supposed beliefs.

Examine the two examples of the Christian priesthood that we are given in the play – Fray Valverde and Fray De Nizza.

Valverde's faith is rigid, uncompromising. Notice how he accuses Atahuallpa and his High Priest Villac Umu in Scene 4 of deliberate stupidity, when they question some of the beliefs and rites of the Catholic Church. He sees Satan in these people, and is determined to crush him at all costs.

Fray De Nizza appears, initially, to have a more sympathetic and flexible faith. Look at his explanation of the love of God to Atahuallpa. He tells him that for love to flourish and grow it must be freely given, not ordered. Atahuallpa, he declares, commands his people to adore him; God *asks* his followers. Decide, however, whether you feel that the priests are truly asking the Indians to follow God, or whether they are not, in fact, behaving like Atahuallpa and ordering them to do so.

Notice, too, that De Nizza also sees the presence of Satan in the Indian society. Its very order, its fixed equality, its sameness, are sources of evil and destructiveness for De Nizza. There is no physical hunger, so no one struggles to improve their lot. There is no emotional hunger, so no one strives for self-improvement. Atahuallpa's attempt to make all men equal, De Nizza asserts, has resulted in the suppression of individuality. Sufficient food, adequate shelter, and an ordered life are not enough, the priest declares, to satisfy the inner needs of the individual. Remember how De Soto approved of the Indian society. Consider whether either society is preferable to the other, or whether neither provides the total answer.

In Act 2, Shaffer develops the analogy between Atahuallpa and Christ. In Scene 2, Atahuallpa declares that he has 'been on earth thirty and three years'. He does not say, 'I'm thirty-three', but 'I *have been on earth* thirty and three years'. Remember that Christ was thirty-three when He was crucified. Similarly, Atahuallpa does not doubt that he is the son of the Sun God, just as Christ believed His own divinity.

Consider why Pizarro should so wish the Inca King to be immortal. In Scene 7, Pizarro likens his situation to being trapped in a cage, longing for a gaoler to set him free. His cage is his body, which is relentlessly ageing, and which will ultimately die. Compare his image of himself to the similar description De Nizza gives to Atahuallpa in Scene 4, of man's body as a prison. De Nizza believes that God's love is the gaoler, the agent, which frees mankind from the temporal shell of his body. Notice, however, that Pizarro does not want Christ's vague promise of happiness and immortality after death. If Atahuallpa is the immortal god he purports to be, then he can give him immortality on earth, he can conquer Time and make him live for ever.

When the State and Church declare that the Inca King must die, Pizarro is adamant in his opposition. How, he asks, will the world know that he, Pizarro, conquered Peru, if they are all killed, as they assuredly will be if they execute Atahuallpa? Do you believe this to be the only – or the real – reason for Pizarro's determination that Atahuallpa must not perish? Remember that Atahuallpa was the first man who had ever made Pizarro display the very human emotion of laughter. Note, too, that Atahuallpa's death causes Pizarro to cry for the first time. Though the Inca King has not given him immortality, he has made

Pizarro truly human and caring at last. Now Pizarro longs for his own death, for the peace and oblivion that only death can bring him.

Assignments

1 'Which character or characters in the play would you describe as being a figure/figures of tragedy?

Suggestions for your answer:
Trace the development of Martin throughout the play. Notice how idealistic he is at the beginning of the expedition. What does he desire most at this stage? Remember who warned him that his ideals were too high. Which incident shatters his dreams and illusions? What do you feel he loses, when he no longer has any ideals? Examine his own words at the beginning of the play, and at the end of the play. Is Martin a tragic figure?

Examine Atahuallpa. Is his life and/or fate tragic? Does his character alter at all throughout the play? Consider his conversations with Pizarro, and then compare them with the conversations he has with the other Spaniards. What is different about them? How much of his tragedy is due, not to his horrific death, but to his misguided trust in Pizarro?

Did you feel that Pizarro is a tragic figure? Examine his character, his life. Can you understand his dreams, his aspirations? How much of his unhappiness is due to his own nature, and how much is due to forces outside his control? Is Pizarro's tragedy the fact that he is alone and rootless, the fact that he longs for something that no one can ever have, or is it a combination of the two?

2 Why do you think Shaffer included the character of Martin in the play? Say what you think his function is.

3 Imagine that you are one of the soldiers who goes with Pizarro on his expedition to Peru. You have been asked by a newspaper to send home occasional reports on the expedition. Write a report covering a particular incident in the play. It could be when the soldiers massacre Atahuallpa's followers, or when the gold begins to arrive and the soldiers start to fight over it, or the death of the King himself. You should include your opinions of Pizarro. Is he wilfully endangering your life, or is he right to protect the King when he has given his word?

Tom Stoppard

Tom Stoppard was born Tomas Straussler in Czechoslovakia in 1937, the son of Eugene and Martha Straussler. He and his parents moved to Singapore in 1939 when his father, who was a doctor, was appointed to a post there. During the Japanese invasion of Singapore Eugene Straussler was killed, and after the war Martha married Kenneth Stoppard, an officer in the British army. Tomas took his stepfather's surname and adapted the English spelling of his own Christian name to become Tom Stoppard.

Stoppard's most noted works to date are *Rosencrantz and Guildenstern are Dead* (1967), *The Real Inspector Hound* (1968), *Jumpers* (1972), *Travesties* (1974), *Dirty Linen* (1976), and *Night and Day* (1978).

As an exponent of Brecht's theory of alienation (see pp. 2–3) Stoppard goes to extreme lengths to ensure that his audience are well aware that what they are watching is a performance. *The Real Inspector Hound* contains the theatrical device of a play within a play and then Stoppard intertwines the two actions so that it becomes difficult to tell what is 'real' and what is 'fiction'. *Rosencrantz and Guildenstern are Dead* includes excerpts from Shakespeare's *Hamlet* which are intermingled with Stoppard's original dialogue. The most notable features of Stoppard's style, therefore, are the sudden and unexpected twists of action he employs, and amusing and penetrating parodies.

Stoppard's characters are generally the victims, the second-rate in society. As an Absurdist (see p. 9) Stoppard portrays them as lacking any power or influence in the face of forces beyond their control. They are lost and alone in societies which not only do not understand them, but also, because they are not 'winners', do not value them either. A reading of T. S. Eliot's poem 'The Love Song of J. Alfred Prufrock' shows clearly one of the sources of Stoppard's inspiration for his characters. The poem depicts the thoughts and emotions of Prufrock, a middle-aged man, who realizes that he is never going to be a hero, never going to be in the forefront of the action in anything. He is one of life's ordinary, undistinguished mortals, and that has been his allotment in life. Nothing that he can do will change his destiny.

The Real Inspector Hound

On the stage set a singularly poor and quite unintentionally funny 'whodunnit' is being acted. The chief characters in this play are Lady Cynthia Muldoon, the owner of the house where the action takes place, her husband's crippled half-brother Magnus, Lady Cynthia's friend Felicity Cunningham, the cleaner Mrs Drudge, an uninvited house guest, Simon Gascoigne, and the policeman, Inspector Hound.

Birdboot and Moon are two theatre critics who have been sent by their respective newspapers to review the 'whodunnit'. Birdboot is more interested in the charms of the actresses than in the play itself, considering himself, quite erroneously, as a 'star maker'. Moon is not his newspaper's premier critic but the second string to Higgs, whom he wishes were dead so that he could have his job.

During a pause in the 'whodunnit' the stage phone begins to ring. It is Birdboot's wife Myrtle wondering where he is. Before Birdboot can return to his seat from the stage set the play recommences, not with a new scene but with a repeat of the scene the two critics have already witnessed. This time, however, Birdboot finds himself cast in the role of Simon. Birdboot, as Simon did before him, finds the body behind the settee but is horrified to discover that it is Higgs, Moon's boss, not an anonymous actor. Like Simon, too, Birdboot is shot, but this time the impression we have is that the shooting is not theatrical but actual.

Moon goes to Birdboot's aid and becomes similarly enmeshed in the plot of the 'whodunnit', cast in the role of Inspector Hound, while the actor who played that role, together with the actor who played Simon, take the two critics' seats in the audience.

Previously, Inspector Hound interrogated the actors but now Moon becomes the prime suspect when Magnus reveals that *he* is the real Inspector Hound in disguise, so Moon must be an impostor. Moon recognizes the actor playing Magnus as Puckeridge, his understudy at the newspaper, but before he can escape Puckeridge, disguised as Magnus and Inspector Hound, kills him.

The requirements of the 'whodunnit' have been fulfilled and Puckeridge has also elevated himself into the position of first-string critic, a position he plainly always wanted.

Act 1

Notice how Stoppard cleverly parodies the genre of the 'whodunnit'. The 'whodunnit' Birdboot and Moon watch is full of clichés, like the obligatory isolated country house which can, when fog opportunely rolls in, become cut off from the rest of society, and the char, Mrs Drudge, who continually supplies the audience with completely unsolicited information regarding the backgrounds of the characters in the play. The upper-class tennis playing characters, who speak in a stilted, artificial language and deliver clues with the finesse of a sledge-hammer to the effect that they all have motives to commit murder, are similarly clichés. All these facets of the 'whodunnit' are quite legitimate, but consider what happens when Stoppard piles them one on top of the other. The atmosphere required for a successful 'thriller' is completely shattered, and we begin to laugh at the incongruity of it all.

Examine how Stoppard also parodies the theatre critics in the forms of Birdboot and Moon. When they speak to one another about their everyday lives and experiences, they engage in 'normal' ordinary conversations. Look, however, at what happens when they decide to give their opinions on the merits of the play. Suddenly, their expressions become full of pompous exaggeration which in no sense reflects the true calibre of what they are watching. As in the parody of the genre of the 'whodunnit', some of the expressions used by the critics – the references to Sartre, Pinero, the outsider in society – are not, in themselves, ridiculous. What creates the humour is that this very poor play patently does not bear comparison to the references made.

Notice that Birdboot and Moon are also *personally* parodied as critics. None of their opinions is original or personal. Neither of them seems to have a single, independent thought in his head. The hotch-potch of literary jargon and philosophical catch-phrases they cobble together are clear examples of their shallowness and ignorance. The height of achievement for both men appears to be how much of their reviews are reprinted on posters outside the theatre. Poor Moon has never managed to have more than a few words used, whereas Birdboot has had virtually his entire review in lights. The irony of this is that Birdboot isn't even particularly interested in the theatre or acting. He judges the actresses on the stage purely upon how accommodating they are prepared to be towards him off-stage, rather than on whether they can act.

Though there is much humour in the play, notice that there is also contrasting pathos, particularly in the character of Moon, the perpetual also-ran. Birdboot's first words to him are to ask where his superior Higgs is, and Moon wonders sadly whether that question will be engraved on his tombstone, as it is constantly asked of him. Despondently he wonders when all the other second strings, the understudies in the world, are going to rise up and supplant those in whose shadow they seem doomed perpetually to live.

Consider that, ironically and horrifyingly, Moon's dream actually comes true. It is not Moon, however, who comes out from the shadows, but his junior Puckeridge. Puckeridge becomes not only the 'hero' of the 'whodunnit' in his character of Magnus/Inspector Hound supposedly unmasking Moon as the murderer, but also a 'winner' in eliminating the two men who stood in his way at the newspaper.

Parodying theatre critics and parodying the genre of the 'whodunnit' are not Stoppard's only aims in the play. He cleverly blends the two parodies so that the audience is left wondering what is true and what is not. Look at how he achieves this ingenious intermingling of the two actions.

The on-stage prop telephone becomes a real one, so that when Birdboot goes to answer it he is trapped on the stage.

Scene 3 does not follow scene 2 – we see the second scene again. Notice here that although the actors and actresses say virtually the same lines as they did before in Scene 2, coincidentally (another theatrical convention), Birdboot's replies actually fit in with the plot.

In the 'whodunnit' Simon had an affair with Felicity, but then decided that it was Cynthia he really loved. Remember when Birdboot and Moon were talking about the play in their audience seats, Birdboot asserted that he would make Felicity a 'star'. Later in the play, however, when he saw the prettier Cynthia he, too, changed his mind and switched his allegiance.

In a conventional 'whodunnit', too, not all the characters are what they initially appear to be. Magnus, the disabled half-brother of Albert Muldoon, Cynthia's long-lost husband, is in fact Inspector Hound in disguise. He pretended to be Magnus in order to trick the real murderer into returning to the scene of the crime disguised as Hound in order to shoot his second victim, Simon. Magnus is not only Inspector Hound in disguise but also Albert Muldoon who had conveniently lost his memory and also – in order to link the 'whodunnit' play and the critics' 'play' – Puckeridge disguised as all three.

The two plays have mingled and merged to become one, but consider whether this play is any more 'real' than the other two. At the end of the play, we see the bodies of the two critics lying, apparently dead, on the stage set, but are they dead, or is this another red herring so common to the 'whodunnit' convention? Notice, however, that by ending the play in this manner, Stoppard has not only used Brecht's alienation theory to its full limit, but has also shown us how uncertain our terms of reference can be. We cannot be certain about what is 'real', and what is not, any more.

Assignments

1 Why do you think the characters of Birdboot and Moon appear more 'real' to us than the actors and actresses who appear in the 'whodunnit'?

Suggestions for your answer:
Examine, first, the 'whodunnit' characters. Look closely at their dialogue. Do you have any sense of these characters having had any 'past', any independent existence, outside the lines they are given to say? Do they have any relationship with the other characters in the 'whodunnit'; do they have any future when the play ends? Consider whether the fact that the 'whodunnit' is not very good influences your opinion of these characters, or is that unimportant?

Look now at Birdboot and Moon. What do we know of them, as characters, from their dialogue? They talk about their work, Birdboot's wife, about trivial matters unconnected in any way with the play they are watching, about their hopes and dreams. Does this give them a greater sense of reality? Do you care about what happens to them? Notice, too, whose perspective the 'whodunnit' is seen from. Consider whether this makes Birdboot and Moon seem more 'real' to us. Notice, too, that when Birdboot and Moon become part of the 'whodunnit', Birdboot's words only fit in, by sheer chance, to what everyone else is saying, and Moon's do not at all. Why do neither of them lose their 'reality' when they become part of the other play? Is it because you are more interested, you care more about their fates, than you do about the other characters?

2 Write a character study of Moon and Birdboot, comparing and contrasting them both.

3 Write a short story as though you were Puckeridge, in which you reveal why you decided to murder your superiors. Give your personal views of Moon and Higgs, what it was that you envied about their jobs, whether you feel guilty now, or elated, at what you have done.

Many of the themes explored in *The Real Inspector Hound* are also present in *Rosencrantz and Guildenstern are Dead*. After considering the methods used to critically examine *The Real Inspector Hound*, use similar methods to consider the following assignments.

Assignments on Rosencrantz and Guildenstern are Dead

1 Consider why Stoppard does not make Shakespeare's two characters 'heroes' in his play.

Suggestions for your answer:
Remember, that having taken these two characters from *Hamlet*, Stoppard has two alternatives. He can transform their natures, but, if he does so, he will have to create an entirely new plot. Alternatively, he can work within the confines of an already established plot. In choosing the latter course, what advantages does this have for Stoppard? Do you feel, indeed, that the plot element is the most important thing, so far as Stoppard is concerned? Look at the main themes of the play – predestination, the 'losers' in life, the essential loneliness of mankind, the absurdity in life. Is Stoppard interested in 'winners'? Look at the play's structure. Notice how, by creating a life for Rosencrantz and Guildenstern, outside of their original roles in *Hamlet*, Stoppard emphasizes their isolation even more. They seldom know what is happening and no one ever bothers to tell them.

2 Do you feel more sympathy for Rosencrantz or Guildenstern

in the play? Try to explain clearly why you feel as you do.

3 Rewrite the end of the play in a short scene, in which Rosencrantz and Guildenstern become 'winners'. Perhaps they could destroy the letter, and rise to eminence at the English court. They might not go to England at all, but begin a new life somewhere else. Which character do you think would take the initiative, take the first step towards controlling their own destinies? Would they, perhaps, decide together?

Further questions on modern drama

1 *An Inspector Calls*, by J. B. Priestley, is a play with a message. Explain how this message is conveyed.

Suggestions for your answer:
Notice how Priestley creates the illusion that the Birlings are just an ordinary family, who are celebrating the engagement of their daughter, Sheila, and Gerald Croft. This is deliberate. We are not to see the family as in any way unique, but just like you and me.

Initially, Sheila and her brother Eric, Gerald, and Mrs Birling are very sketchily drawn. Sheila appears much like any other young girl who is very much in love with her fiancé. Her brother Eric drinks too much but, despite that, he resembles most brothers in his teasing of his sister. Gerald is polite, cultured, and rather one-dimensional. Mrs Birling could be any businessman's wife, as she supports and encourages her husband, interrupting him only when she feels he is talking too much.

Mr Birling, conversely, is very much centre stage from the very beginning of the play. He speaks, and his family – and we – listen to his pronouncements on politics, business, the possibility of war, and life. Priestley makes no direct judgement on Birling's views, but encourages us to draw our own conclusions.

Consider how much of Birling's life revolves around monetary concerns and public opinion. While delighted that Sheila is engaged to Gerald, much of his pleasure is governed by the fact that the marriage will merge his and Gerald's father's businesses. Look at how proud Birling is of having created his own business, and yet consider how that business flourished. Women, like Eva Smith, were paid appallingly low wages and, if they attempted to better their situation, they were sacked. Birling, however, is not interested in what the people work for him think. He is only concerned with his own society's opinion. Nothing holds terror for him except the thought of a public scandal attached to his name. Notice how often he repeats the view that the most important consideration in life is to look after one's self and one's family. Initially, Mr Birling's views do not seem particularly harsh, and certainly not evil.

Inspector Goole is the catalyst who creates the play's dramatic action, and the judge who unlocks the true natures of Eric, Sheila, Gerald and Mrs Birling. Through each character's interview with Goole, we learn of each individual's values, and we learn the play's message.

Sheila is not the simple, innocent girl she appeared. Deliberately and maliciously, she had Eva sacked from Milward's because she was jealous of her. Of course Sheila did not think her actions would have such dreadful consequences, but it is Priestley's opinion that she *should* have thought. Sheila is horrified by Eva's death, but compare her reactions with those of her father. He tries to intimidate the Inspector and, when that fails, to excuse himself from blame, although he sacked the girl from his firm.

We are made to see quite clearly that neither Sheila nor her father is individually to blame for Eva's suicide. Such a judgement would be too easy. Gerald, Eric, and Mrs Birling, must also be shown to have been at fault, so that Priestley's theme of mankind's collective responsibility can be reinforced.

Gerald used Eva, enjoying his role as her protector until he tired of her, and then discarded her. Eric, like Gerald, manipulated Eva for his own gratification but – unlike Gerald – he does show true remorse at the results of his actions. Notice that Inspector Goole reserves his most scathing attack for Mrs Birling, who arrogantly appointed herself as Eva's judge at the Brumley Women's Charity Organization. Mrs Birling, as a woman and a mother, should have had compassion, should have extended pity and help to Eva, but she turned her back on her. For Goole/Priestley, this is unforgivable.

Consider how much we know about a character we have never seen. We know what Eva looked like, what her nature was, how good and selfless she was. We are not, however, simply to feel pity for someone who is dead and beyond our help. As Inspector Goole reveals, there are millions of people alive who are just like Eva and who need our help and consideration.

This could have been the end of the play. Each character feels guilty at the part they have played in a girl's death. Priestley, however, not only has a deeply pessimistic view of mankind, but also wants to extend his message directly to us. We look on, with disbelief, as Mr and Mrs Birling, and Gerald, worry only about how to avoid a public scandal. When they discover that there is no such person as Inspector Goole, and no girl has been brought into the hospital as a suicide, any feelings of guilt they had are supplanted by feelings of relief. For Sheila and Eric, such considerations are unimportant. Even if no girl died, this doesn't alter the fact that they have all admitted to individually treating *a* girl abominably. The 'twist', of course, is that the phone call at the end of the play reveals a girl *has* died, and a policeman is being sent to interview them.

Priestley makes it clear that *we*, the audience, are not to think that because none of *our* actions have caused someone's death, we are therefore blameless. Our actions may not have such appalling results as we discover in the end that the Birlings' had, but our actions *do* affect others daily.

2 *The Fire Raisers* Max Frisch
Notice how much of the play's impact depends upon the creation of feelings of fear and menace. How does Frisch create these emotions? How, too, is the play as much an examination of societies, as it is of individuals?

3 *Sergeant Musgrave's Dance* John Arden
Show the effect the arrival of the recruiting sergeant and his men has upon the miners, and on characters like the Mayor, Annir, and Bludgeon. What particular issues are we being asked to consider in this play?

4 *A Taste of Honey* Shelagh Delaney
Do you feel the play is an optimistic or a pessimistic one? By referring to some of the characters and situations they face, explain why you feel as you do. Examine the dramatist's use of setting and dialogue. What impression do you feel Shelagh Delaney is trying to create?

5 *The Dragon* Eugene Schwartz
Examine the play's portrayal of people's political behaviour. Does Schwartz seek to influence the reader towards a particular viewpoint?

6 *Under Milk Wood* Dylan Thomas
Which characters did you find most memorable, and why? What impression do you feel Thomas wishes the reader to have of Llareggub and is he successful in achieving his aim?

7 *The Winslow Boy* Terence Rattigan
Is there one particular character you felt most sympathy with in the play? Say why you feel as you do, and how you think Rattigan achieves this effect. How much of the play is intended to be a criticism of society's values, as well as an examination of individuals' attitudes?

8 *Murder in the Cathedral* T. S. Eliot
Write an account of your reaction to the character of Becket. How does Eliot's dialogue, and the attitudes of the other characters in the play, influence your opinion?

9 *Arms and the Man* George Bernard Shaw
Describe the principal characters, and explain how Shaw encourages us to examine quite serious issues through a vehicle of comedy. What aspects of society do you think Shaw is making fun of?

10 *The Admirable Crichton* J. M. Barrie
Trace the development of the main characters from the beginning of the play, through their time on the island, to when they return to 'civilization'. Which – if any – of the characters, do you think have gained most lasting benefit from their experience?

11 *Mr Bolfry* James Bridie
Examine the conversations between Mr Bolfry and Mr McCrimmon. What opinion does Bridie intend us to form of the character of Mr McCrimmon from these conversations, and how does he shape our attitudes?

12 *The Long and the Short and the Tall* Willis Hall
Compare and contrast this play with R. C. Sherriff's *Journey's End*. What similarities in attitude, style, characterization, social grouping, do you see? How do the two plays differ from one another?

13 *Rhinoceros* Eugene Ionesco
Consider how the dramatist creates feelings of hysteria, menace, and fear, from a situation that appears, initially, to be farcical. Why does Ionesco not portray his character, Béranger, as a conquering 'hero'?

14 *Chips With Everything* Arnold Wesker
What do you find most moving about the situation, and the characters, in the play? Examine the dramatist's very particular use of setting and dialogue, and explain what you think his intention might be behind this.

15 *Who's Afraid of Virginia Woolf?* Edward Albee
Which of the characters most attracted you, and why? How does the dramatist persuade us to alter our sympathies as the play progresses? Consider how the dramatic tension is created in this play.

16 *The Plough and the Stars* Sean O'Casey
Consider the ways in which the play is both comic and tragic. Compare, and contrast, the characters of Bessie Burgess and Fluther Good, and explain how they contribute, in different ways, to the overall impact of the play.

17 *Indians* Arthur Kopit
What disturbing issues are we being forced to examine in this play? The play does not follow a chronological sequence. What, do you feel, is the dramatist's intention behind this?

18 *Becket* Jean Anouilh
Compare, and contrast, this play with T. S. Eliot's *Murder in the Cathedral*. Clearly, the style is very different, but in what other ways do the two dramatists' portrayal of the historical event differ, and in what ways are they the same?

19 *The Flies* Jean-Paul Sartre
Describe the incident that you feel is the climax of the play. What do you feel is at stake at this point? Is the conflict resolved as you felt it would be, and how did you react to the various characters at this time?

20 *A Voyage Round My Father* John Mortimer
Write a clear account of the plot, as briefly as you can. What is it about this play that makes it so appealing? What, do you feel, are the distinctive traits of each of the principal characters?

21 Adapt *any* of the above questions to a play you are studying but which has not been named here, and write an answer to it referring to your chosen play.

Further reading

The Angry Decade Kenneth Allsop, Peter Owen 1959

Mid-Century Drama Laurence Kitchin, Faber 1962

Anger and After John Russell Taylor, Methuen 1969

English Drama: A Modern Viewpoint Allardyce Nicoll, Harrap & Co. Ltd 1968

Twentieth Century German Literature Harry T Moore, Heinemann Educational Books 1971

The following Brodie's Notes are available on
individual play texts cited above:

Pinter: Three Plays (*The Birthday Party*/*The Homecoming*/*The Caretaker*)
Who's Afraid of Virginia Woolf?
A Man for all Seasons
A Taste of Honey
Murder in the Cathedral
The Crucible
Death of a Salesman
An Inspector Calls
Hamlet
King Lear

In addition, there are Brodie's Notes on the following plays:

A Midsummer Night's Dream
Antony and Cleopatra
Julius Caesar
Macbeth
Othello
Romeo and Juliet
The Tempest
Twelfth Night
Doctor Faustus
The Duchess of Malfi
The Glass Menagerie
Pygmalion
Spring and Port Wine
A Streetcar Named Desire